Messengers of Infinity

SUNY series in Contemporary Continental Philosophy

Dennis J. Schmidt, editor

Messengers of Infinity

On the Pictorial Logic of Leonardo da Vinci

EYAL PERETZ

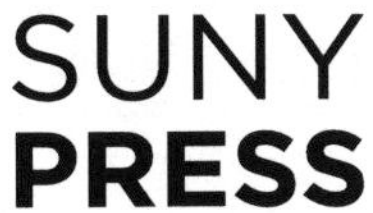

Published by State University of New York Press, Albany

EU GPSR Authorised Representative:
Logos Europe, 9 rue Nicolas Poussin, 17000, La Rochelle, France
contact@logoseurope.eu

For information, contact State University of New York Press, Albany, NY
www.sunypress.edu

Library of Congress Cataloging-in-Publication Data

Name: Peretz, Eyal, author.
Title: Messengers of infinity / Eyal Peretz, author.
Description: Albany : State University of New York Press, [2025] | Series:
SUNY series in Contemporary Continental Philosophy | Includes bibliographical
   references and index.
Identifiers: ISBN 9798855801545 (hardcover : alk. paper) | ISBN 9798855801552
   (ebook) | ISBN 9798855801538 (pbk. : alk. paper)
Further information is available at the Library of Congress.

Contents

Introduction

At the Threshold of Appearance:
Painting beyond the Sacred

In front of us, a painting. As we approach it, a complex set of attractions and withdrawals occur. On the one hand, it seems to call us out of and away from ourselves, toward it and into the world. Yet at the same time, even as the painting draws us in, thus becoming most intimate to us, it seems to pull away, as if receding further and further from our grasp. We are left on our own in an isolation that can be in turns mournful or joyful. Thus, as we draw toward it, toward the world, the painting withdraws from us and we withdraw into ourselves, as if cut off from the common world, even exiled.

I am not speaking here of any specific painting. All real images circulate around the question of this mysterious and complex experience—an experience we can understand as that of *fascination*—of being drawn toward that which withdraws. Examples are legion. They include cave images, where this experience is presented figuratively, through scenes of hunters chasing sacred animals, which withdraw from them in the struggle between life and death each seems to face alone; or medieval images of Christ, whose invisible aspect becomes paradoxically present, as it were, *as* precisely that which is withdrawn from the icon; or the great Chinese landscape paintings, which, even as they draw us into their distances and depths increasingly seem to withdraw from us, covering themselves in foggy mystery, leaving us isolated inhabitants of a realm totally opaque to us. It extends too to cinematic images like the shadowy figure of Orson Welles's Kane, who, the more he withdraws into his enigma, leaving the world with his secret, the more we are drawn to him, fascinated by him as one through whom each of us faces alone our own singular enigma. Or even to those bewildering images we call dreams, which withdraw into oblivion the more we try to hold them fast, like Eurydice from Orpheus's gaze.

It is the background contention of this book that a history of images (of which we will examine one fundamental moment, the work created by Leonardo at a pivotal point in the Western development of painting) can be written from this perspective. In such history it is a question of following the different ways that the complex experience we have sketched above, the experience of fascination, the being drawn by that which withdraws from us, comes to function within the general conception and aim of the image. While I believe that all real images,[1] in every culture and in a number of specific ways, revolve around this enigmatic event of calling-out and withdrawal, of self-loss and birth into the world, briefly, of transfiguration and metamorphosis, this book focuses on the specific shift from medieval Christian *sacred images* to Renaissance or early *modern painting*, as it reaches its most rigorous articulation. In the works of Leonardo, *every* aspect of painting comes to be subjected to the question of the nature and significance of this shift.[2]

Both sacred Christian imagery and Renaissance painting, I argue, constitute the moment in the history of images in which the question of fascinating withdrawal began to open up as an explicitly *logical* problem, namely, the problem of what unifies the whole: in both, a new kind of demand for unity appears that will draw together each and every aspect of the image, from the size and distribution of the figures to the division of the pictorial space to the position of the spectators to their eye movements in relation to the painting. The pictorial surfaces of medieval sacred images and Renaissance painting are logical surfaces or logical spaces, that is, spaces governed by a new kind of centralizing, unifying demand. While it might be the case that some images of previous eras were also conceived in relation to a demand for unification, what is new in Medieval sacred images and Renaissance paintings is that that around which they circulate in their totality, or in all their aspects, is a withdrawal. It is the withdrawal that unifies, or it is the withdrawal that functions as a call for unification.[3]

The fact that the question of withdrawal, which, I claim, has always accompanied all images, comes to function, first in the sacred image, then in Renaissance painting, as a logical problem around which a visible surface starts to unify itself is the result of many complex factors of which I will mention a few. First, there is the introduction of a Greek philosophical sensitivity into the question of the image, through one of its fundamental terms: the logos. From a philosophical point of view, the logos is in essence what is withdrawn, or at least a different dimension from every actual thing. For, by definition, logos is not any specific thing but that which names a dimension of a whole, something beyond all phenomena, within which each and every actual thing or phenomenon take their place. Second, there is the revolutionary introduction into the world of a new conception of the whole through the discovery/revelation of the Jewish God, itself now fully understood as a mystery withdrawn from the world, yet dominating the *whole* of the (actual) world. Third, there is the appearance of the Christian understanding of Christ *as* logos, attempting to fuse the Greek conception of the whole with the Jewish one inscribed in the withdrawn God. This fusion culminates in the conception of a privileged, exceptional worldly actuality that nevertheless, paradoxically, stands for the dimension of the logical, that is, stands for the whole that is enigmatically withdrawn from every specific actuality, a paradox—Christ—for which the name Image will be needed (and Christ will thus be simultaneously Image and logos). Only through the combination of all these factors can a visible surface start to arise that sees itself as a privileged, paradoxical phenomenon, a visibility that serves as the place of inscription, or of a "showing," of *an invisible withdrawal* in which the demand for a whole, thus for a unification, is inscribed.

This demand for unification governs, first, each and every aspect of the pictorial surface itself. Second, by foregrounding this new logical demand for unity, the pictorial surface comes to stand as an anchoring point for a much more encompassing demand for unity characterizing existence as a whole. Since the logos indicates that there is a dimension of a whole in relation to which each and every specific phenomenon, or everything that sensibly appears, comes to stand, the emergent logical task of the pictorial surface is not only to display or exhibit its own specific unity but also to serve as a privileged, paradoxical phenomenal site from which the call to unify the whole of existence is uttered. Medieval and Renaissance pictorial spaces are thus literally phenomeno-logical spaces where the whole of existence is at stake.

Ultimately, though, what is most essential about the shift that medieval sacred imagery introduces into the history of images is not that it foregrounds a whole governing existence; after all, many ancient images often held a cosmic function, displaying, for example, a harmony (sometimes mathematically calculated) that supposedly permeates the whole or served to show the place of the gods who control the world. Now, however, displaying the whole was understood phenomeno-logically. What this means is that the pictorial surface becomes the site for the display of the distinction or difference between two dimensions: the dimension of visibility or phenomenality, of every possible thing that comes into appearance, and the dimension that is withdrawn from phenomenality in principle, that can never itself have any positive appearance but whose withdrawal is the background of our *opening to* any and every appearance, the dimension of logos, newly understood following the complex history briefly sketched above. The logos is now that withdrawal from appearance and visibility *through which* we open to any and every appearance, to the whole *of* appearance.

The ultimate mystery within the context of this understanding of the image that emerges with medieval sacred imagery is not an absent god or ghost or any other fantastically exceptional positive appearance but rather a paradoxical appearance, one which is a regular appearance, in the sense of belonging to the everyday realm of perception, yet in which withdrawal as such is inscribed. Such appearance paradoxically *appears as withdrawn*, but in such a way that its withdrawal discloses an ultimate withdrawal *through which* the whole (of appearance) opens, namely, discloses logos. In this sense, the image still retains a dimension of exceptionality—which characterized traditional images as sites for the appearance of gods or sacred, otherworldly, beings—and is still to be understood as an exceptional appearance, but one whose exceptionality is no longer a positive one, but is rather the exceptionality of something that can never be just an everyday appearance since it is that which stands *at the threshold of (the entire realm of) appearance*, thus is that in whose withdrawal is inscribed the power of opening to appearance. If withdrawal, in such a context, is inscribed in specific figures, they are to be understood as liminal figures, thus as being neither regular, everyday, worldly appearances, nor supernatural beings that can somehow make an appearance in the image, but those standing at (regular, everyday) appearance's enigmatic threshold.

Each and every resource of painting, the totality of the aspects of pictorial space, henceforth serves to activate and show this threshold. Indeed, we can say that the difference between subsequent pictorial periods, as well as between individual artists and various theories of art, will consist in how they actualize or interpret the general question of what the threshold of appearance consists of and entails. Thus, for example, to mention some of the most familiar and oft-discussed analyses, we can think of Michel Foucault's famous examination of Velasquez's *Las Meninas* and of the Subject during the "Age of Representation": the enigmatic threshold figure, the sovereign outside the space of any actual depiction, who "appears" in the painting only as withdrawn from it or in being absent from it. By the same token but along opposing lines, consider Jacques Lacan's examination of anamorphosis in Holbein's *The Ambassadors*, which poses the question of the gaze as the inscription in the painting of the place of the subject's horrifying vanishing point, the place of death—which also lies outside the actual space of representation. In the gaze it is not the question of representation's sovereign constitution, as in Foucault, but that of its anxious limit and threat of its collapse, and we can thus say that at the threshold of appearance, which the image as inscription of the gaze shows, is the disappearance and collapse of (the Subject of) representation. Or we can think of Michael Fried's discussions of absorption in modern painting, where the absorbed pictorial figures he analyzes are those that, by constitutionally refusing us and withdrawing from us, create a new space of immanence, sufficient unto itself, a dimension with no outside, or perhaps more accurately with no actual outside. Such absorbed withdrawal that ignores anything actual outside the space of the painting seems to aim at the elimination of a *wrong experience of the threshold* of appearance: one occupied by a theatrical spectator (a Subject of representation) outside the actual representation for whose pleasure (or manipulation) a scene is constituted—a (falsely theatrical) scene, possibly a world picture, in the sense Heidegger gave the term, characterizing for him the condition of modern subjectivity. By being drawn in by what withdraws from us and refuses or ignores us, we, those who behold the painting, lose our capacity to hold the position of theatrical spectators securely occupying an actual outside (subjects of a world picture made for our pleasure, benefit, and domination) at the threshold of appearance. In this sense, painting liberates us from the false theatricality of the world picture.

In medieval sacred images, the figure of Christ harbors the greatest mystery: he is the very paradigm of the threshold. In him is inscribed the withdrawal that never appears but opens the realm of appearance as a whole. The conceptual sources at the background of the *pictorial* Christ's coming to hold such an exceptional phenomeno-logical place at the threshold of appearance are found in the theological tradition wherein Christ is understood both as logos and as image, in the writings of Saint Paul and Saint Augustine, for example. Christ is thus the paradigm, in the interpretation of the pictorial tradition whose aims belong to the Christian tradition even if they do not necessarily fully coincide with it, for a phenomenal site that inscribes the invisible and withdrawn logos, displaying this logos in the world and through this display making us open to the question of the whole in us and our place in the whole. Every pictorial image in this sense will have

Christ the Image as its point of reference and model, and every pictorial image will aim to function as *a* Christ, in a way, namely, as a phenomenological exceptionality, or will aim at least to serve as displaying the logic of Christ with its own probably insufficient earthly means, functioning as the threshold between phenomenal appearance and invisible logos.[4]

Articulating the question of the image as revolving around a split between a logical demand[5] uttered from an invisible dimension and a phenomenal surface whose each and every aspect stands under the authority of this demand, medieval sacred images thus developed a new logic *of* the phenomenon, *of* appearance and the visible. As such, they introduced a radical transformation into the thinking and making of images.

To a large extent, however, given the domination of theology as a framework through which artists understood their own activity, the sacred image's interpretation of the excessive dimension of non-phenomenal logos and its demand for unity was inflected in a specific way. The principle of Divine Reason provided the conceptual framework, which stipulated a grounding, foundational, centralizing, hierarchical spatio-temporal order. Thus, the phenomeno-logical dimension of the image was coopted by or at least put in tension with a theological interpretation of its nature and function. In this scheme, Creation is a hierarchy descending from the highest and most perfect, which is itself invisible, to the lowest, which is visible, guided by a providential order that is seen as a given and from whose unifying power everything flows. In this framework, the image serves as the "threshold messenger": the exceptional appearance that leads into this non-phenomenal hierarchical ordering power and discloses its providential nature. At the center of the image, an image the task of which is to inscribe the logos, will be placed that which most particularly functions as the visible representative of this supra-phenomenal ordering, and which we most properly can regard as the threshold figure, the messenger of the beyond. As Joseph Koerner has remarked of a Bosch altarpiece: "Bosch not only marks the midpoint with some special element in the picture's composition; he also connects that element, by way of its centered mark, to a divine architecture transcending the painting's fiction. Flanked by paradise or hell, beginning and end, archē and telos, the center receives in Bosch an absolute foundation."[6]

Most importantly, the image of Christ serves as the crux between the dimension of phenomenal visibility and hierarchical providence, or divine architecture. The image in fig. I.1, for instance, a representative Byzantine mosaic, enjoins us to look up to the ceiling, which in turn points to heavenly heights in the invisible realm to which all phenomena are hier-

Figure I.1. Mosaic of Christ Pantocrator, Basilica of Saint'Ambrogio, Milan. *Source*: Wikimedia Commons, CC BY 3.0 DEED, Sailko.

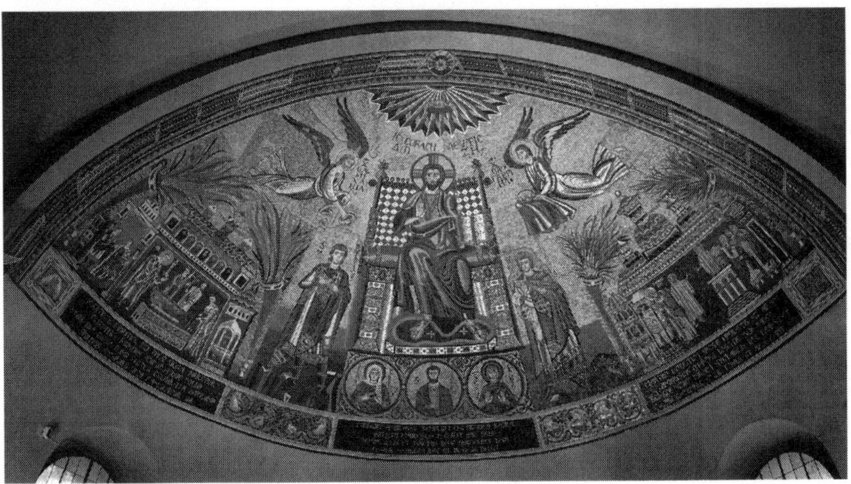

archically subjected. At the top is a beaming solar crown, which pulls us, as it were, beyond the figures toward the edges of the painting, beckoning us to traverse them. Through the central figure of Christ, which is larger than the elements that flank and surround it, our gaze is fitted to a spatial order organized in a particular direction: from top to bottom, from large to small, and from divine to earthly. Likewise, in terms of temporality and its particular circular logic in this image, everything begins with the central figure of Christ, which first captures our gaze. After taking in the angels, then the saints, then the earthly context with its trees, grass, and architecture, our gaze is drawn to him again. Christ serves both as foundation and ground of existence and the final point of rest in an eternal order within which we are to find our place.

At the same time, this theological inflection implies a substantialist ontological dualism, indicating a relation between two realms, the earthly, visible one and the transcendent invisible one. The representation of Christ functions as the visible part of a cosmic architecture that extends into invisibility, creating continuity between the physical and metaphysical realms; the effect is that the dimension beyond visibility is understood with the means characterizing phenomenal space and time, even if it is presumed to transcend them. The metaphysical high is in continuity, even if it is invisible, with spatial height; the transcendent beyond, though infinite in size, remains somehow in relation to the increase in size characterizing the phenomenal figures, and so forth. The beyond is thus a substantial, if invisible, beyond, forming a continuity with worldly substances. A continuous hierarchy of creation exists descending from the invisible to the visible, a hierarchy into which we are to be inserted with the means of the pictorial surface, which here serves as the transitional, mediating site between the beyond above and the phenomenal below. We come to use our eyes in such a manner that they become informed by the invisible beyond perception and are thus allowed to see according to the whole (and to find our place within it).

The Atheological Image

Renaissance painting in general and Leonardo's in particular interrupt the theological arrangement and its ontological dualism. We no longer find ourselves in a closed world in which continuity prevails between high and low and providential temporality directs the whole of Creation from the outset. Like every major event, Renaissance painting transforms *everything*—that is to say, not any particular detail, many of which remain the same as in Christian imagery, but the nature of the whole that it aims to introduce us into. The most celebrated aspect of the new conception of the whole is associated with the invention of perspective, of which Erwin Panofsky's account remains the most famous. In *Perspective as Symbolic Form,* he argues that the introduction of Renaissance perspective involved a new principle of unity guided not by the laws of optics or natural perception so much as by those of a mathematics that in fact distort everyday perception. As in medieval images, the Renaissance pictorial surface serves as site for showing a split between a nonphenomenal, metaphysical logos, on the one hand, and a phenomenal dimension. In contrast to medieval images, however, the metaphysical dimension that the pictorial surface displays is no longer a substantial, providential, and hierarchical divinity, separate from this world; instead, it is now a question of laws of geometry, which are *immanent* to the world, even if somehow foreign to our natural perception. Renaissance perspectival pictorial surfaces, in this sense, are characterized not by perceptual illusionism but by the correction of illusionism (in a similar way to the famous Cartesian project of the correction of the senses that mathematics enables). Paintings are *supposed* to feel foreign to the habits of ordinary perception, opening us to reality beyond illusion, as geometrically guided.

Whether Renaissance painters were animated by belief or treated religious themes is irrelevant: their medium now stands in the service of geometry rather than theology.[7]

What Leonardo discovers in full, perhaps for the first time, is what we can call the dimension of the image proper, beyond its theological and geometrical takeover. Leonardo releases the image, as it were, into a logical dimension of its own, the dimension proper to it. This release, or liberation, which implies the *birth of painting* in its modern sense, builds on but radically transforms the logical achievements of medieval sacred images and early Renaissance pictorial perspectivism. The pictorial surface after Leonardo (at least in possibility, if not always in actuality) is a systematically conceived phenomeno-logical surface of a new kind, one we might properly associate with phenomenology in the modern sense of the term, namely, having to do with exploring the dimension of unity that opens us to a *world of appearance.*

The dimension of appearance in the modern, phenomenological sense is neither the hierarchically lower, sensible realm nor an illusory dimension onto which our senses open, which needs to be corrected. Rather, modern appearance concerns the way that what our senses open us to is understood as showing itself out of itself as it truly is. When things show themselves out of themselves as they truly are (that is, when the dimension of truth is sought not in a realm behind appearance but in the very fact of appearing), they do so against a certain background. This background—which is neither a transcendent grounding substance, nor a cosmic order, nor a mathematical ordering—has received the name *world*, newly, that is, phenomenologically, understood. When things truly appear, they do so in the world, and the world itself—which is the unity inscribed in everything that appears qua showing itself in the ("one") world (or uni-verse)—is nothing but the unpredictable and incalculable openness of things to each other, an openness that they all commonly, equally, and thus democratically share. In this sense the world is not a ground or foundation but what we can call a *medium*, the dimension of the in-between. The world as medium is that mutual openness in between all appearances with the means of which or through the mediation of which everything comes to share in a common being (common appearance) with each other.[8]

To appear, then, is to appear in the world, and through the medium world, to come to show oneself, always unpredictably, on the background of its openness. Yet the world itself, the background to and medium of all that appears, does not itself appear—at least not in the manner of everything that appears "in" (or "against") it. This is where the question guiding Leonardo, the painting as a phenomenological surface of a new kind, enters. As we have seen, the task of the *pictorial* phenomeno-logical surface in medieval images was not to show the visible—the phenomenon—itself but to turn a specific type of space into an exceptional site at the threshold of appearance, in which what shines through is the *unity* at the background of all phenomena, which itself is invisible, or nonapparent. The phenomeno-logical[9] task of the medieval pictorial surface was thus paradoxically to "show" the invisible and nonapparent. Part of what was at stake was to make this invisibility that which comes to *inform our vision* as we look at the image, or more precisely put, as we start to look with the means of the image, with the image coming to serve as our medium. For medieval sacred images, as we have seen, such invisible unity was (at least partially) understood and pictorially practiced as a sort of hidden architecture within which the dimension of the visible took its hierarchically assigned place and we, in our turn, were called to take ours.

Leonardo, as I have suggested, sets out to explore invisibility of a new kind, the "world" in the modern, phenomenological sense. In many ways, he is the first, or at least among the first, fully formed *painter of the world* in the context of Western art.[10] To be a painter of the world means establishing the pictorial surface or space as a site whose every resource, and every aspect, is dedicated to showing a new type of unity, that of the "one" world (or universe), which is the background to, and the medium of, every appearance but which itself is in essence withdrawn from appearance and visibility, and can thus be thought of as an invisibility. As I have argued, the invisibility proper to the world as background of appearance, which the pictorial surface is now dedicated to showing—in the sense of making it that which informs our vision—is nothing other than the openness (thus is not some substantial absence) of everything to everything else without any preconstituted terms, an openness in which everything that appears democratically participates. Painting after Leonardo is not simply the site where phenomena show themselves out of themselves, and thus not in relation to any transcendent foundation or geometrical principle serving as ground. Rather, it is the site where, *in order* for phenomena to show themselves, the invisibility, the nonappearance, of the openness that is the world becomes the active medium informing our vision and thus, in a way, itself comes into view. If the world-as-medium implies the democratic, nonhierarchical openness of every phenomenon to every other phenomenon, unconstrained by any pregiven measure or order, and if painting is the site through which this medium is activated, the modern work of art must be constructed in such a way that it obviates the emergence of a center and a foundational ground in relation to which everything is to be hierarchically ordered; in a sense, this new framework sets us on the course of *ceaseless movement*. The construction of painting as a site for such ceaseless movement lacking a foundational center is indeed Leonardo's aim.

Exceptional Figures in an Infinite Landscape

Understanding invisibility as the openness of the universe (or one world) of appearance means that it can no longer be viewed as occupying some transcendent place beyond the visible; instead, it is nothing but the beyond *of* (in the sense of the medium of) the visible.[11] As such, it haunts the very fact of appearing, silently accompanying every aspect of visibility as a sort of an internal limit to perception that, at the same time, makes perception possible in the first place. If the pictorial surface is to show this background invisibility, the medium, it must be constructed in such a way that it does not separate the two loci of the visible and the invisible; invisibility permeates it *everywhere*, accompanying every aspect of its visible surface as its mute background openness.

This demand to construct a zone that invisibility permeates everywhere underlies Leonardo's fundamental innovation: to equate the entirety of the pictorial space with a new, modern kind of openness, an openness he associates with the landscape.[12] For Leonardo, the landscape is no longer an earthly setting of secondary importance for a primordial sacred drama, as it had been in medieval images, but rather a new kind of opening where the hierarchical, *vertical* distinction between the above and the below is eliminated in favor of a *new horizontality*; here, everything that appears does so on the background of an indeterminate and infinitely open horizon.[13] This invisible openness *is* the modern landscape. What is new in the modern landscape is not a kind of content—say, that of nonhuman nature—but an atheological *medium of appearance*.

Leonardo's earliest known sketch, *Landscape Drawing for Santa Maria Della Nave* (1473), often considered the first "pure" or independent landscape in Western art, exemplifies this basic insight. In this sketch the pictorial surface in its entirety revolves around the appearance of the landscape, the opening of a realm wherein everything that appears does so on the background of immanent, infinite, and horizontal invisibility. From this work onward, all that appears on the pictorial surface does so within that openness that the medium of the landscape enables. Informed by this horizontal openness, our eyes meet the image in a novel way: they roam across it as if on a new adventure, exploring it with newfound freedom.

Leonardo's most famous pictorial technique, *sfumato* (the subtle shading and gradations of tone that result in the blurring of forms and outlines), stands in the service of this new openness. By blurring limits and dissolving the contours of things and figures, it makes everything in the painting lose its fixity and introduces a thorough sense of indeterminacy. The figure or thing blurred by *sfumato* lacks a fully determined context within which or in relation to which it achieves completed form; rather, it is an incomplete element of that openness proper to the landscape. This dimension of essential incompletion and indeterminacy is at the source of Leonardo's leaving many of his works unfinished. Probably for the first time in Western painting, this is a matter not of accident but of principle.

Leonardo's other decisive gesture involves his transposition of the sacred figures associated with medieval painting into the new logical framework of the landscape. Medieval sacred figures, above all Christ and Mary but also angelic beings, served a double purpose, laden with internal tension. Although they were paradigmatic exceptional figures by virtue of the fact that they did not simply belong to everyday appearance, and as such were located at what we have been calling the threshold of appearance, theology and the work of sacralization co-opted the phenomeno-logical project of the image, as we have seen. In their theological and sacred form, such figures as Christ and Mary stood at the center of a cosmic, providential architecture, and the threshold they occupied was understood as the place of separation between two ontological levels: the invisible transcendent and the visible worldly, the above and the below.

In inserting the very same threshold figures into the new context of his painting, Leonardo is not simply secularizing them but releasing them to their full phenomeno-logcal mystery. If *Mona Lisa* is in many ways a transposed Mary, we cannot characterize her as a secularized Madonna; a much more enigmatic quality is evident. Likewise, the Christ of *The Last Supper* is a threshold figure of a new kind. Leonardo's transposed Christ and Mary exemplify something close to what Giorgio Agamben has called *profanation* (which also resembles what Jean-Luc Nancy has called a "deconstruction of Christianity") and has explicitly distinguished from secularization.[14] "Secularization," writes Agamben, "is a form of repression. It leaves intact the forces it deals with by simply moving them from one place to another. Thus the political secularization of theological concepts (the transcendence of God as a paradigm of sovereign power) does nothing but displace the heavenly monarchy onto an earthly monarchy, leaving its power intact."[15] By contrast, to profane is not simply to move things from their place of sacredness, their separation from the everyday world (standing as they do at the transition between the earthly and the divine) into the common earthly realm, but to dismantle the system responsible for the divisions between two ontological realms. In going beyond the distinction between sacred and profane toward a new existence for which we lack a name, Leonardo's paintings, I claim, fundamentally announce and serve as messengers of such existence beyond the division of religious and secular, of heavenly and earthly, an existence that he associated with the medium of landscape, hence their essential *conceptual* significance—a significance that is a focus of this book.[16]

If, in Christian imagery, threshold figures served to divide and connect the two realms, the above and the below, then releasing these figures into the full potential of their phenomeno-logical mystery entails transforming their function. They no longer occupy the space between separate realms but stand at the threshold of the universal openness that the landscape signifies. In this capacity, they function as heralds of a new *world of appearance*, inscribing and activating its withdrawn, nonappearing background. As we will see, we can also think of these threshold figures as *messengers of infinity*, whereby infinity characterizes the realm with a horizon that lacks measure and predetermination within which all finite phenomena appear.

Enigmatic withdrawal characterizes these messengers (whether Christ, the Mona Lisa, Anne, or the angel from Leonardo's *Annunciation*). What withdrawal means within this new, worldly framework is that these threshold figures do not belong to their surroundings; they cannot be located in any specific context, and they defy a precise time or place *within* the landscape. Announcing the landscape's infinite opening, these figures radiate a mysterious power, the power at the heart of their withdrawal, the power of being beyond any specific appearance or determinate time-place. This beyond is not the metaphysical beyond of sacred painting, indicating a hierarchically higher invisible realm, but a *beyond* (understood as medium) *of any appearance*, a beyond belonging to appearance in the sense that it is nothing but appearance's or visibility's invisible background. Thus, the mystery of the Mona Lisa is that she cannot be located with any precision within the landscape, seeming to be separate from it. Better put, she is herself the landscape as such, *as medium*. To be withdrawn from any specific place in the landscape means to be inscribed with the power of the landscape as medium. Similarly, in *The Last Supper*, the open window behind Christ marks his connection to the landscape. No longer the medieval Christ occupying the center of a cosmic hierarchy, he is a modern Christ, standing at the threshold of a new, nonhierarchical open community expressed in the dispersed, disorganized plurality of the apostles. Though still central, his centrality is transformed, for it no longer functions as a call for a cosmic orientation but as that through which everyone in the nonhierarchical community, first of all the apostles, and then we together with them, is infused with that infinite background of the landscape's opening. Christ's centrality is now the centrality of the medium: he is the gateway to the new world with the means of which our eyes and our life are now called to open.

One last aspect of Leonardo's achievement is crucial at this juncture. Around these messengers of infinity another adventure looms as the inseparable shadow of the world-as-infinite-landscape: the surreal world of dreams, nightmares, erotic desire, and everything else that later came to be associated with the realm of the unconscious. Withdrawn from any specific time and place, these enigmatic figures at the threshold of reality are also those which open us to, or open within us, the dimension of dreams, for it is this dimension that occupies the mysterious threshold between visible reality and its immanent invisible background. Dreaming occurs at that nonplace irrupting at the heart of reality when its immanent background—infinite and unpredictable openness—suddenly flashes and "appears" on its own, a flashing that also occurs at the moment of the pictorial image as the paradoxical showing of invisibility. We can understand this *nonplace* beyond phenomenal, perceived reality—an immanent invisibility belonging to the visible, to be distinguished from the substantial metaphysical beyond—as *surreal*: the surreal is neither phenomenal reality nor a metaphysical substantial reality beyond, but the mysterious realm that is (at) the threshold *of* reality. In a medieval context, the infiltration into this world of the hierarchically higher invisible beyond would have been understood as the arrival of a mystic vision; now, however, it signals the emergence of a surreal dream.

Having discovered the new medium of the landscape as heralding a new immanent invisibility, an invisibility belonging to the visible, Leonardo in one stroke announces the double birth of modern painting at the threshold of appearance: as newfound realism (showing that shows itself out of itself) and as surrealism. This duality is the hallmark of these enigmatic images he has bequeathed modernity and that continue to call us to simultaneously open to a world beyond the sacred and the profane, the religious and the secular, and to our profoundest, ever-withdrawing, dreams.

Chapter One

The Annunciation of Painting

Falling into the Landscape
(*The Annunciation*; *Virgin of the Rocks*)

It all starts with an angel . . .

According to Vasari's famous account, Leonardo's master, Verrochio, asked him to paint one of the angels for his *The Baptism of Christ* (1472–75) (fig. 1.1). When Verrochio saw the result, he was so incensed by his pupil's achievement that he decided to stop painting from that day forward. Leonardo's angel, we might say, announced something new, something that exceeded his master's capacities and—even more important—his vision, which marked the birth of a new idea of painting and, with it, a new way of conceiving what is at stake in the task of painting. Yet what, precisely, did this angel that so troubled Verrochio announce? The first painting usually attributed to Leonardo, *The Annunciation* (1472–75) (fig. 1.2), represents, I suggest, an initial attempt to provide an answer. We can understand the work, the theme of which is the announcement by an angel of a miraculous birth, as itself the miraculous birth of Leonardo into painting, having received the gift of painting from the angel. More still, the work brings out a new interpretation of the significance of Christ (who could be understood, following Pauline tradition, as the redeeming image) for the question of painting.

The angel Gabriel is an otherworldly emissary announcing to the Virgin that she will conceive a child who is an incarnation of the divine. As such, Leonardo's painting seemingly presents itself by and large as a traditional Christian painting, offering us in the form of a pictorial narrative the miraculous event at the heart of Christianity. Within the context

Figure 1.1. Verrochio Baptism of Christ, detail. *Source*: Wikimedia Commons, CC BY-SA 4.0 DEED, Livioandronico2013.

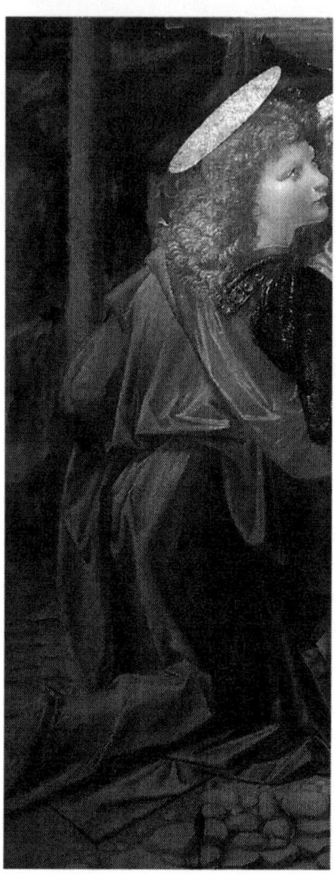

Figure 1.2. Leonardo, The Annunciation. *Source*: Wikimedia Commons, CC BY-SA 4.0 DEED, Livioandronico2013.

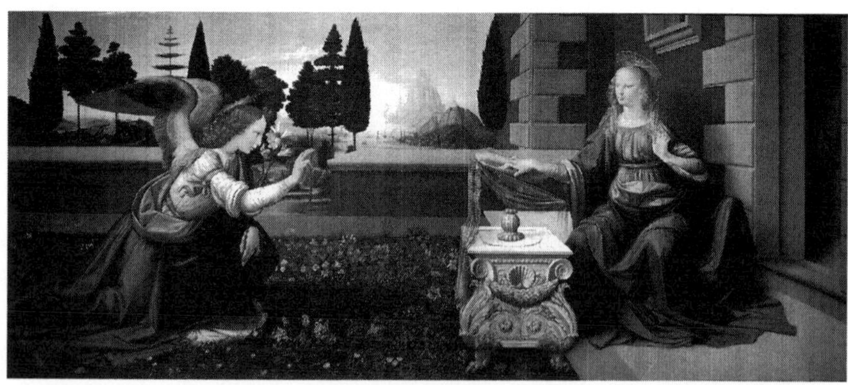

of this traditional scheme, the painting itself, a physical, earthly thing, is understood as a repetition of the original announcement (and miracle) in that it consists in the coming into appearance, into the world, of that whose nature is divine and invisible. The angel of annunciation is a patron saint of sacred Christian painting, and each sacred painting is thus a sort of earthly birth that repeats—and receives its legitimacy and raison d'être from—the original Christian miracle. Yet even as Leonardo's painting draws from this traditional scheme, taking advantage of the allegorical relation it establishes between the theme of the annunciation and the question of painting, it already confronts us with a very different landscape, both pictorially and affectively, and develops, as a result, a very different conception of painting that is now to be associated with the theme of the annunciation.

Perhaps the most immediate indication of "trouble" is precisely the landscape itself. We cannot miss the two central characters as we gaze into the painting, but our eyes are nevertheless drawn away from them, into an increasingly receding distance—a distance that occupies the center of our line of vision. An opening in the trees at the exact upper center of the painting interrupts what we can understand as a natural mechanism of framing, thus of limitation, which the trees would otherwise form.

As a result of this opening, the spectator is drawn in uncontrollably, without arrest, since the painting's mysterious depths have no precise limits and lack a definite horizon. One all but drowns in the misty sea that appears as the ground vanishes. The painting poses a stable set of delimiting coordinates in a geometrically organized space: a rectangle inhabited by the two figures (especially the Virgin, seated at an enclosure); but it also effaces these contours, notably through the technique of sfumato (the subtle shading and gradations of tone that result in the blurring of forms and outlines), for which Leonardo is celebrated. The passages of sfumato dominate the space outside the rectangle, with its circular and windy paths, leading us on a way of ever-increasing indeterminacy, growing mistier and almost blank the further we meander.

This captivation of our gaze by the hazy and infinitely receding landscape means that the figures themselves, the protagonists of the traditional Christian drama, relinquish their centrality as the coordinates around which the painting revolves. It is as if they become subservient to the landscape. Unlike in earlier paintings of the Annunciation where the landscape (if one exists) serves to indicate an earthly context into which a sacred drama is introduced, pointing us away from earthly existence, here the drama turns out to be the drama of those who belong to a landscape, or the drama of *coming* to belong to a landscape. The annunciation in Leonardo's painting thus becomes first of all the annunciation of a new kind of landscape, or the announcement of the birth of a new kind of image opening as such a landscape, a landscape that infuses our gaze with a captivating infinity, a blank indeterminacy. The angel is, from this perspective, not the messenger from another world but the messenger of the landscape, or even, from the point of view of pictorial technique, the messenger of sfumato.[1]

Unlike the Virgin in her enclosed corner, the angel appears *within* the landscape. His head and wings, which rise above the wall, almost seem to have been painted on the landscape, or even to form part of it. The wings seem to appear on the background of an earthly sky rather than a heavenly one, a sky marking the landscape as an indeterminate openness. The angel's hand, performing a portentous gesture, is located at the aperture in the wall that leads from the geometrically framed and enclosed garden toward the landscape beyond, as if to say, "I am come to deliver you from here," from a delimited, framed space.[2] We can see that the painting as a whole is composed of a series of *interrupted* frames—the opening in the garden wall, the window, as well as the door (both of which are cut off), the interrupted tree line, and so forth. The angel points toward an indeterminate, possibly risky and disorienting landscape that can end in drowning yet extends the promise of a strange new freedom.

As a messenger of the landscape, of a newly opened earthly realm, the angel has fallen from a heaven to which there is no return. Indeed, we might say that the angel has lost his heavenly wings, a fact indicated by Leonardo's famous and unprecedented gesture of giving the angel naturalistic wings, modeled on birds of prey, instead of showing them in pure, incorporeal color (as in Fra Angelico's *Annunciation*, for example). This does not mean that the angel is now to be understood naturalistically, that he is not a messenger of a beyond.[3] Rather, I will try to show that the angel here still manifests a beyond, but it is a beyond of a new kind, an *immanent* beyond that no longer adheres to the theological schema of traditional angels.

Returning to the question of the wings, we can add that the angel's wings become—much like in another story of a falling angel, an angel giving up his heavenly wings, which Wim Wenders has authored—wings of desire. For it is a story of a new kind of desire that opens here, in that the fallen angel becomes, among other things, a protagonist in what is undoubtedly an extraordinarily complex erotic drama centered on a scene of seduction. The Virgin here, in slight contrast to previous depictions, does not appear surprised or frightened by the unexpected apparition. In her almost blank and impassive expression, a new kind of blank stare (not yet but already quite close to Manet's *Olympia*), she appears to hover between a waiting, even an unnamable longing, and a state of apprehension, possibly even traumatic frozenness or shock. The angel of the landscape seems to be coming in response to the Virgin's erotic dreams, even as he is someone touching on her nightmares, taking the shape of a menacing bird of prey. He is a shadowy stranger, a figure mixing beauty and horror (and beauty is very much the beginning of horror in Leonardo). His large and projecting shadow, almost like a stain on the painting's surface, intimates the possibility of violence coming from a place beyond conscious grasp.

We are not far from the world of Kleist's *The Marquise of O* and its investigation of a conception that never becomes available to the heroine's consciousness. In the novella's famous, enigmatic ending, the Marquise explains to her husband her earlier flight from him, after having learned he is the one who, unbeknownst to her, violated her: "throwing her arms round his neck, she answered that she would not have seen a devil in him then if she had not seen an angel in him at their first meeting." A fantasy of heavenly descent, the creation of an idealization that aims to eliminate an erotic horror, having been tinged with a mysterious sexuality (occurring in our painting in the staining shadow) has transformed the one who occupied the angelic place into a horrifying devil.

The communication between the dark, bloody red worn by the angel in the painting, the Virgin's pink, and the pink bed cover we glimpse through the shadowy opening behind the Virgin's back, which itself communicates with the angel's shadow, creates a virtual trajectory of violation that might or might not give us the Virgin's imaginary space. It is this line of violation that turns the angel in the Virgin's eyes into a predator.

The angel, then, plays an ambiguous function. He is suspended (and it is a clearly gendered, masculine angel, as I discuss below) between serving as the messenger of the landscape—a new way of opening up to the world, which he brings to a cloistered Virgin in what seems to be a theologically structured space that belongs to a tradition of painting Leonardo is in the midst of interrupting—and being a dark and shadowy stranger playing a role in a scenario of seduction that is astonishingly precocious in its grasp of the workings of what later came to be known as the unconscious and its relation to sexuality, a precociousness we usually associate with Romantic artists of the late eighteenth and early nineteenth centuries. Both aspects of what we might call the modern angel, worldly on one hand, libidinal, or psychoanalytic, or unconscious, on the other, emerge from the dissolution of the theological angel and its heavenly announcement. The resulting mystery is Leonardo's signature style, achieving in perfect and inextricable balance a new vision of the world, a new kind of realism, and a new, in many ways surreal, dream world hovering over the abyss of a nightmare (a dream world that seems very different from the still theologically natured *visionary* world of someone like Giotto, for example). Leonardo is not an artist for whom life is a dream, but one for whom life is an exposure to a landscape, an exposure always accompanied by, and inextricably linked to, a shadowy dream. The angel is the precise point of contact within this inextricable synthesis of a new realism and a new surrealism, between the discovery of the world and the discovery of the unconscious (which is the shadow of the world, the absence that gives a ghostly presence to the world's indeterminate openness), and as such the announcer of all the possibilities of the modern, post-theological world to come.

This coming together of two elements—the announcement of a new relation to the world (which now opens as a landscape with indeterminate, effaced horizon) and of a new shadowy realm that seems to circulate around dreams, nightmares, and eros—around the figure of the angel inscribes itself in a particularly fundamental and enigmatic way in the strangest visual element in the painting, the shadow cast by the angel. Located at the very place, in the very distance, of the occurrence of the annunciation, thus the space between the angel and the Virgin, in many ways this shadow *is* the annunciation.

On the one hand, of course, the shadow can be explained as a gesture of realism. It is after all the cast shadow of the angel on the grass (which by itself already carries the implication that the angel is a fallen one, his presence subject to the earthly laws of appearance). Yet the intrusive prominence of the shadow—its very noticeable presence as a sort of formless stain, which is almost disturbing in its introduction of darkness or the negation of visibility in the context of what is otherwise a clear collection of elements composing the area of the framed and mostly evenly lit garden—suggests that something more is at stake.

The shadow is positioned within our line of vision exactly in continuity with the opening in the garden wall/frame and the exposure that it introduces to the infinitely receding, blank-becoming landscape. This would seem to indicate that the shadow is to be considered precisely in relation to this exposure—indeed, as the shadow *of* this exposure. It is as if the shadow, the taking away of visibility, or the encounter with the negation of visibility, were the flip side of the opening of a new kind of visibility announced by the infinitely receding landscape. Or as if the "condition" of the gaze opening in us, a gaze through which we are exposed to the landscape, is that of suffering a blind spot, an effacement of any content. What does this mean? It means that the landscape as Leonardo understands it is that which opens in relation to a gaze for which there is no determined horizon, no actual limits or determinations that will satisfy it and exhaust or fulfill its function. The blind spot, which appears as a shadow, is the erasure or the effacement, the absence of any given determination, an erasure that is the condition of opening to a landscape. The shadow/blind spot is a nothing at the heart of the gaze, an absence of predetermination of the aim of the gaze, a gaze that is thus pure, anxious openness lacking any given limit or direction.

We can understand the nothing inscribed in the shadow as what announces a new beyond, a beyond I have called immanent. The beyond is no longer, as it was in the theological schema, a substantial, invisible dimension separate from the visible realm. Rather, it is the nothing (of determination), which is the condition of the opening of this world. We can also think of it as the "invisible" background to the visible realm, in the sense that it is not a content *in* the world that opens but the very event of its opening out of nothing (out of no preexisting determination). This immanent beyond is thus an invisibility *of* the visible, proper to the realm of the visible, an invisibility that is nothing but the indeterminate opening of visibility.

This immanent beyond, inscribed in the blind spot that is the angel's shadow, *is* the angel's annunciation, what the angel now brings into the world, a world no longer opposed to a substantial metaphysical beyond. If the traditional angel, and the conception of the image that accompanied it, announced a metaphysical beyond in order to draw us to that beyond, and away from the world, what the modern angel announces is a world in which, or to which, the beyond is immanent. The modern angel is no longer the messenger of a substantial beyond but a figure who stands at the *enigmatic threshold of this world*, the inscription of the world's opening out of nothing (determinate).

We have seen that the angelic annunciation, which takes place in and as the shadow, heralds not only the world as landscape but also a new kind of scene of seduction. In this light, a novel understanding of the mystery of eroticism emerges, as well as the attendant mystery of birth and impregnation. If, ever since Plato's *Symposium*, eros had been understood to mark a relation to the beyond, the eros announced in Leonardo's painting is also to be understood as the trace of the beyond; in the latter, however, this beyond is no longer an eternal elsewhere outside the actual world but the very beyond that is the event of opening of this world, a world whose heart is nothing: openness beyond any specific determination and direction. Eros is the witness to the world as opening out of nothing, and it comes to inscribe itself in the body as that which is called by the beyond, called beyond itself, called by the world.

According to Christian logic, the angel is a nonerotic figure, even a neutered and neutering figure, who announces an immaculate, thus, unstained, impregnation that has nothing to do with eros. Leonardo transforms this logic: the angel is the call of the beyond *into* eros, and eros itself is the sign of the new, nonmetaphysical beyond. If impregnation is still angelic and miraculous within this new logic as well, it is not because it is nonerotic or nonsexual but because sexuality, or the dimension or the erotic—the dimension announced *in* the shadow, or *in* the stain, a withdrawal from visibility at the heart of the visible—is itself "miraculous," as it involves the arrival out of nothing, out of the world as such, rather than out of something specific *in* the world. The infant announced in this image, and *as* this image, marks an arrival from nowhere in particular, from nothing, namely, from the world as such. This miraculous arrival cannot be explained causally, since causal explanations can be supplied only for things that happen *in* the world, not *to* the world itself. The infant comes to inhabit the body as that which is possessed by the relation to the beyond, namely, by this world in its opening as such. We might say that the painting itself is something by which we, the viewers, have become miraculously impregnated, in that it is the gift of the arrival of an angel, the messenger of the world as landscape. The painting comes to inhabit us, penetrating us through our eyes, incorporated in us, as an angelic message from the beyond. The annunciation is thus that which marks the birth of the world as landscape in us as well as our own birth into the landscape.

But who are *we*, those in whom a landscape is born and who are born into a landscape?

As we have started to see, the angelic shadow also stands for our gaze. This means that the shadow marks our own place in the picture, or the painting. It marks the place of our implication in the painting's opening as a landscape. If the shadow is what we have called a blind spot, an erasure or effacement of any determination (a "nothing"), then we can say that we are those who are stained by an effacement, by a nothing, a nothing through which we become those who come to inhabit a landscape. The shadow is the annunciation of our self as that which circulates around a fundamental effacement or, we can now also say, disappearance, the withdrawal from any determined appearance. We open to a landscape, a realm of appearance that stands under the sign of an immanent beyond, an effaced horizon, because we are those who disappear, thus who lose any determined figure, becoming nothing but the shadow of the world as the beyond. From this perspective, painting inflicts us with a disappearance in order to open us to the appearance of the world as landscape.

Of course, the same is the case for Leonardo, through whose gaze the painting opens in the first place. In this sense the shadow is his self-portrait, the (blind) spot where the artist comes to be inscribed in the painting most fundamentally, albeit in the form of disappearance, as withdrawing from any figuration. Leonardo is the shadow cast by the angel: an effacement brought about by the annunciation of painting as the birth of the world as landscape. Thus, the new conception of painting Leonardo develops, that of painting as landscape, comes together with a new conception and experience of the self, the self as a shadowy beyond. We might describe it as destitute openness, a being reduced to nothing where, through this reduction, one opens to the world. Taking this a bit further, painting means the development of the pictorial surface as the realm through which to engage with, and to bring into enigmatic visibility, the self as a shadowy disappearance, a disappearance that opens us to the realm of appearance as landscape. It is as if only with the means of a new kind of painting that this self, the self as an evanescence, is able to come to appear (as nothing) and occupy a worldly realm, that of the landscape without determinate horizon.

Yet, this means that the pictorial surface now becomes an enigmatic realm where a complex mixture of longing and alienation, desire and home-lessness, is inscribed. The more one makes one's self appear, as nothing, the more one disappears, becoming lost to oneself and to the world, unable to give oneself any recognizable or identifiable figure and place. The more one appears, as shadow, in the world, the more the world as a habitation, a place of determined identity and belonging, withdraws, becoming something like the inhospitable and inhuman desert depicted in Leonardo's *Saint Jerome* (fig. 1.3), an early work more or less contemporaneous with the *Annunciation*.

This is the problem of the landscape: the more one is exposed *to it*, the less one is able to locate oneself *in it*; as such, the painting, by means of which one is born into the landscape, but as lost and disappearing, is a realm of an intense desire and search for belonging. Restated, it poses a question: how can one find a place of habitation and belonging when every possible and determined horizon of existence has been taken away?

Figure 1.3. Leonardo, *Saint Jerome in the Wilderness*. *Source*: Wikimedia Commons, CC BY-SA 1.O DEED, universal public domain dedication.

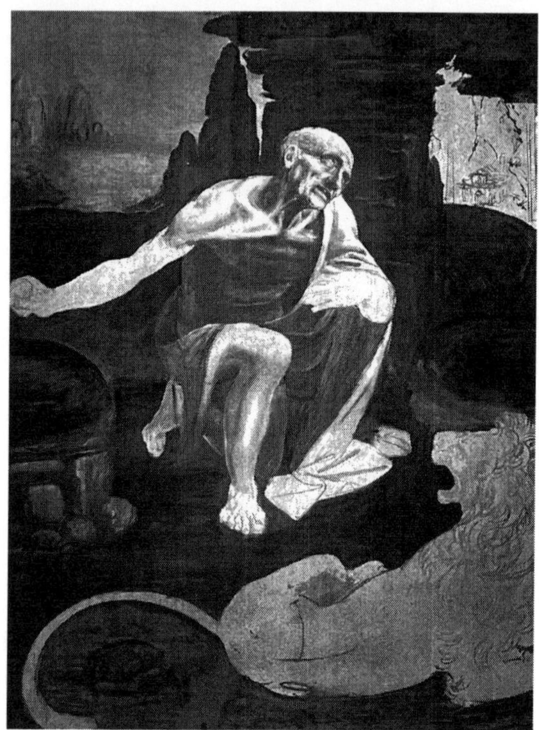

A Home in Exile

These seem to be the questions animating Leonardo's first major work completed in Milan (1483–86), his new place of habitation a few years after the execution of *Annunciation*, following his self-imposed exile from Florence and the professional home of Verrochio's workshop. The painting, known as *Virgin of the Rocks* (fig. 1.4) is traditionally interpreted as a moment of exile: a portrait of the Holy Family, significantly without the father figure but with an additional infant, John, on the way to Egypt.

In *Virgin of the Rocks*, we are no longer in a garden but fully and immediately within the landscape. In consequence, the function of the figures occupying the painting in relation to the problem of the landscape is somewhat different. As a methodological principle, to read any of Leon-

Figure 1.4. Leonardo, *Virgin of the Rocks* (the Louvre version). *Source*: Wikimedia Commons, CC public domain.

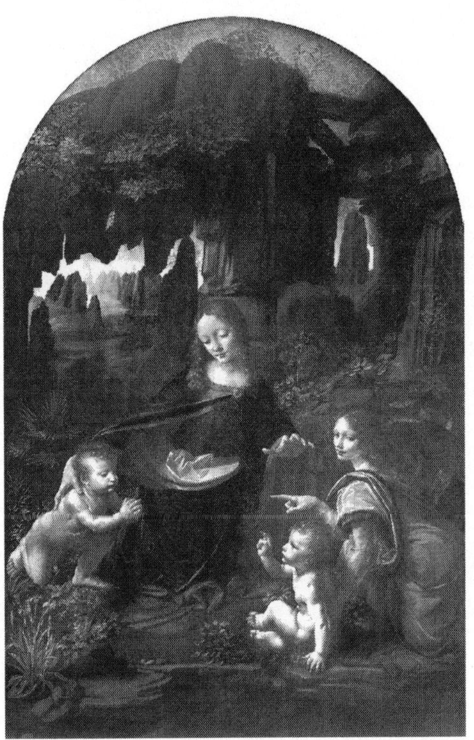

ardo's major figures, be it Mary, Christ, or Mona Lisa, is to see how they are informed by the problem of the landscape: what modality they occupy as receivers and communicators of the landscape's announcement. Indeed, it seems to me that the unprecedented beauty—a beauty of a new kind—of this painting is that it is perhaps among the first Western paintings that is worldly through and through. The problem of the world, the *idea* of a world or of the landscape, fully informs every figure occupying the pictorial space and every gesture of which the painting is composed. It is important to emphasize that by "worldly" we should not necessarily hear *secular*, if by this we mean the abandonment of any reference to the beyond. For indeed, as we have started to see, the world as Leonardo conceives it, a landscape with an indeterminate horizon, implies a beyond, even if that beyond is now immanent, a beyond (which I suggested should be understood as the medium) *of* this world, which in a way *is* this world, a world that is overcoming the metaphysical division between the world and beyond the world that governed painting prior to Leonardo. The implication of an immanent beyond in Leonardo's conception of the world is thus neither simply a secular realm (which would involve no beyond at all) nor a theological one (understood in relation to a substantial beyond-the-world). The modern image is that wherein this third option is trying to become articulated and to come into view.

The focal point of this coming into view, in the context of *Virgin of the Rocks* and in many ways in Leonardo's work as a whole, is the feminine face, which bears perhaps the most essential relation to the problem of the landscape in that it is the field on whose surface the announcement and message of the landscape is inscribed in its utmost complexity. As we have begun to see, the question of the landscape opens as a relation between an indeterminate horizon and a black hole, associated in *Annunciation* with the shadow cast by the angel. Within the context of *Virgin of the Rocks*, we can associate this same dark withdrawal with the yawning abyss at the bottom of the image. The painting stretches between the indeterminate horizon that opens, by means of *sfumato*, at the top, and the abyssal bottom. At the very center is the face of Mary, in relation to which the three other figures are organized.[4] She thus appears as if torn between being called by the infinity of the horizon and being threatened by its abyssal horror (not unlike the dual sides of the angel's visitation, that is, the concurrence of his alluring beauty and his threatening violation).

Mary's face, then, is the center,[5] the focal point, on which is inscribed in its full weight the *announcement* of the landscape (i.e., the event of the world's infinite opening, the incessant call that is this opening). She is the site of the inscription of that nothing, of that shadowy withdrawal from any determination, which is the "condition" of the opening of the world as a realm with no determinate horizon. We have seen that a fundamental expression of this announcement of the landscape as the event of the infinite opening of the world is the miraculous arrival of an infant, miraculous because it arrives out of nothing. The relation between the withdrawn feminine face, inscribing in its withdrawal that new, immanent beyond, and the miraculous child (first and foremost Leonardo himself) is perhaps the most fundamental configuration through which the problem of the world as landscape opens for the artist. Indeed, this relation haunts a great deal of Leonardo's work.[6]

To inscribe the landscape, we have seen, is to inscribe what we have called the immanent beyond (that which is withdrawn from any determination). The feminine face in Leonardo is thus always withdrawn, beyond. It never establishes a relation of full reciprocity, dedicated as it is first of all to the announcement of the world, in a way belonging to the landscape whose withdrawal and infinite receding it expresses. Marked by infinite recession, the feminine face in Leonardo is conceived as both always drawing us in, inhabiting us as the call of the beyond, yet withdrawing from us, abandoning us, always an evanescence. Mary's withdrawal from the baby Jesus here, her face literally turned away from him even as she is possibly eyeing him from a distance (a distant watching that is both an indication of a painful separation as well as the inscription of a special bond), is a fundamental expression of such withdrawal and abandonment at the heart of which is a fundamental relation, which we can understand as that of a sharing of the beyond, or a sharing through that which always opens an irreducible distance. Mary's withdrawal is registered in two ways: in the gap between mother and infant here, which is—contrary to our expectations—the largest of that between any of the figures and Mary, and in the placement of the infant, who, almost abandoned, is sited on the very verge of the abyss.

Yet, it is not only Mary who is beyond but the infant as well. The infant is first of all beyond Mary, not her infant, as the angelic intervention made clear earlier, but passing through her as an expression of the world, a message of the landscape. As such, in her relation to the infant, it is Mary herself who is abandoned, experiencing an anxious gap. Indeed, there is a double abandonment effectuated from the reciprocal perspectives of mother and infant. It is remarkably expressed in Mary's enigmatically suspended hand, which hovers in the gap. Is the hand withdrawing from the infant, exposing him to the abyss, and thus to a world that has no ground, or is the hand approaching the infant, trying to close the anxious gap that his withdrawal from her opened within her and that has left her exposed to the abyssal landscape? Or is the hand engaged in a gesture of protection, reaching toward the child to save him from falling into the abyssal ground-lessness of the landscape? Or is the hand withdrawing from the infant not by way of simply abandoning him to the world but by way of letting him be on his own, teaching him separation, that is, teaching him the lesson of an originary beyond, the lesson of coming to inhabit a landscape or world without established and guaranteed relations?

The angel, an imaginary figure, comes to occupy this gap created out of the complex tensions of the problem of the beyond as they unfold between mother and infant, enigmatically gesturing from within this space. The angel here (another figure for Leonardo?) is no longer the ambivalent demonic/saintly herald of the landscape but a sexually ambiguous adolescent who arrives from within the tensions of a landscape that has already been announced, in its infinite call and abyssal horror. It is as if the angel, a mysterious presence, points toward a resolution of these various tensions, a solution that might consist of nothing but the painting itself. This role is indicated first by the position of the angel's gesturing hand. Although it leaves the gap between mother and infant open, it at the same time reduces it, mitigating the effect of the horror of its void. Likewise, the angel's other hand holds the infant Jesus, as if to prevent him from falling into the abyss, and serving as the ground that will enable his blessing gesture, which is also a proto painting gesture, as if the hand gesture of the miracle child that blesses out of his abyssal exposure parallels the one of the miracle child who will become a painter.

It is unclear, though, from whose perspective the angel's appearance is to be understood. Is he a messenger coming from the side of the mother's imagination? In this case, the angel can be understood as a memory image of the originary and somewhat scarring event of the annunciation through which she was exposed to the infinite and abyssal landscape (it is as if the angel here is still charged with the erotic and menacing red), a memory image that is reactivated as she experiences the separation from the child. This memory image also serves as something communicated to the child at the moment of separation, perhaps, among other things, as something sent from the mother to protect him at this moment. Or is the angel a product of the infant's imagination, emerging as a power of image-making (or perhaps as an imaginary friend) out of the gap opened by the loss (or abandonment) of the mother, the infinity of her distance? The secret of the angel is that it is probably all of these at once. The angel belongs neither to the mother nor to the infant but is an annunciation of the beyond they share, which is, by definition, beyond both, that which passes between them, an infinity communicated in their abyssal separation, which is also what is common to them, the paradoxical form of their bond.

Yet, what is crucial about the angel, and indeed makes it a figure of resolution, is that though it is a memory trace of the announcement of the landscape, it is a memory trace that has a certain spatiotemporal actuality. The angel becomes something that is somehow *in* the landscape or world, part of it, and not just outside it as the power of its opening. The angel, which stands both for the painting itself and for the strange type of actuality that characterizes the painting, is thus actually present, yet paradoxically so: it exists as what is always beyond, thus as nothing, a fact also indicated by the fact that the angel's robe and wings extend beyond the pictorial frame, and thus beyond any available actuality.

We have seen that there is a fundamental problem for those to whom the landscape is announced: while they become exposed *to* the landscape, to this world and its immanent beyond, they can no longer locate themselves *in* the landscape. The world that appears to them becomes the source of their abyssal disappearance, their horrifying self-loss. The angel, which we can understand as the image, is a kind of solution to this problem. It allows for both the opening of the landscape in its indeterminate infinity but is also the means, or the medium, through which the self can hold to something in the world or in the landscape, thus to itself *as* in the world, yet in the world as open to its infinity, thus also beyond any specific place. The angel or image allows both mother and infant to separate, to open to the beyond that is the world, yet to become present, thus becoming present to each other, not to drown in or fall into the abyssal dimension of the landscape.

The angel's function here could be said to be like that of a valve, a source of fascination for Leonardo in his studies of water, the heart, and the mechanics of breathing, for instance the underwater breathing machines he drew with opening and closing regulating mechanisms. The valve in *Virgin of the Rocks* though is transcendental in nature, as it were, allowing for a regulated transition between the infinite beyond (the medium), which is the world or landscape as such, and the particular place and time the figures occupy. The angel (a transcendental prosthesis, i.e., an artificial mediator of the gap of the infinite) lets the beyond in and regulates the passage of those who are in the landscape to the beyond, in such a way that they do not completely disappear in the process.

Another figure through which we can understand the function of the angel is the technology of flight, which was also of particular interest to Leonardo. The machine he famously sketched consists of a delimited surface, thus an actuality, which yet opens us to the beyond, or to the sky, even as it allows us to have a certain ground; its angelic wings (modeled in fig. 1.5 on wings of bats rather than the birds of prey of *The Annunciation*) are like the surface of a canvas, functioning as a sort of vehicle of the landscape, permitting us simultaneously to open to the beyond yet hold on to something in the world.

The success of this angelic intervention, allowing for the immanent beyond to be accessed, is expressed in the blessing gesture of the infant Jesus. Grounded over an abyss by the angel, the gesture communicates the angel's support and the transformation of the abyssal distance opened through the

Figure 1.5. Leonardo, flying machine. *Source*: Wikimedia Commons, CC public domain.

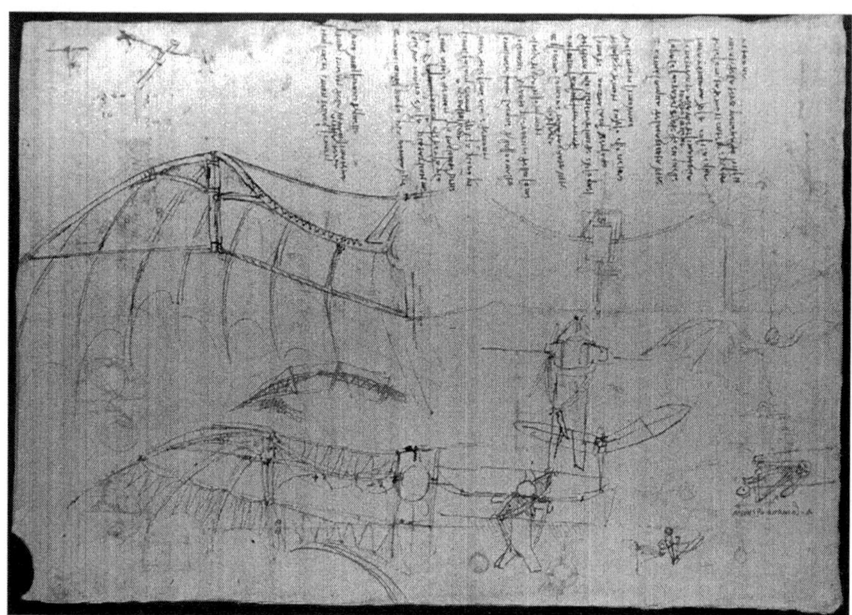

mother. The blessing is the expression of bringing the beyond into the world. The blessing is thus the achievement of the image as that which allows one to open to the landscape even as one starts to find oneself in it.

Such self-finding through the mediation of the angelic image connects here with the problem of trying to achieve a new kind of habitation, a place of belonging, for a humanity for whom the announcement of the abyssal landscape seems to have meant the loss of habitation. For the annunciation of the landscape, as we have seen, also implied an exilic essence of humanity: not belonging anywhere, always disappearing into the shadow through its exposure to an indeterminate beyond or an indeterminate horizon. Finding oneself on the road to Egypt, or Milan, abandoned and unprotected, is the consequence of the announcement of the landscape. The challenge facing these exiled figures to whom the landscape has been announced is both to remain faithful to the annunciation yet to come to be in the world, rather than disappear in its abysses, ending up as roaming shadows. The angelic mediation, as a transcendental valve, aims to resolve this challenge, by allowing for an attachment to specific actualities that, by locally responding to one's exposure, serve as points of orientation and belonging. Thus a certain closure is allowed in relation to the exposure to the infinite beyond, yet it is an enclosure that always leaves one partially exposed, open to the landscape and its indeterminate horizon. The new habitation is neither a total interiority, a closing in on oneself, nor an exteriority, the occupation of a fully exposed outside, but a rocky formation leaving one partially enclosed and partially exposed—a specific actuality in the landscape that keeps us open to the landscape as such, never separating from it in the manner of the enclosed garden from which we started.

Indeed, the rocks seem to inscribe the transformation from the state of finding oneself abandoned in a landscape into a kind of habitation that includes the announcement of the landscape at its very formation, even as it needs to limit the exposure to the landscape's indeterminate infinity. On the one hand, the rocks look like an alien (and alienating) component of a realm from which one feels excluded; their hardness and formlessness seem to reject any accommodation with this newly opened realm. On the other hand, they seem to have turned into a protection of sorts, allowing the exiled to find a certain refuge while still being open to the landscape, to an indeterminate outside that remains a vital part of their habitation. The openness to the landscape that here comes to serve as the very definition and function of painting, as well as of architecture, is not that of a window carved in a fully formed house (through which one can safely look into a geometrically organized world, to use the famous Albertian description) but the coming-to-be of a habitation that is part of the landscape even as it gives one a slightly separate place. As such, it can serve as a perspective *on* the landscape. Such a site allows one to have a place of one's own that is exposed to the landscape yet located in it, and in doing so comes to serve as well as a gate to our dreams.

What enables such a paradoxically separate, yet open, structure is the mystery of the artistic, pictorial frame figured here in the rocks. Cutting them out of their surround, as it were, it grants them distinction through separation, which enables them to serve as a center of orientation: a "local" in the landscape that is one's own, through which one can start opening up to the landscape without disappearing.

The angel is the emblem of such dynamic framing. As we have noted, his wings are cut by the pictorial frame, thus indicating that they stand for the cut, or for the activity of pictorial cutting. In their stony grayness, it is as if they were made of rock—a cut rock themselves. As the cut is a cut of an actual part of the landscape that exposes it to the indeterminate infinity of the landscape, it is thus a perspective *on* the landscape. The angel as image is the cutting power: the mysterious arrival of an actuality serving as a medium of infinity, allowing one to inhabit a landscape, that is, to become appropriated, by means of a specific and concrete distinguished localization, to this world as the beyond. The rocky abode, as well as this painting—created originally for a church, a church whose logic it comes to dismantle or desacralize[7]—is neither an indifferent anywhere, nor a privileged sacred somewhere, but a contingent part of the landscape that has become, by means of the framing cut, a singular place of appropriation whose idiosyncratic formation cannot be separated from the character of those for whom it will become the center of the landscape, the medium of their world, the gateway to their dreams·

From such a partially closed yet newly opened place of habitation emerges a new kind of community at the heart of which is something we might understand as the blessing of children's play. The communicative essence of the painting—to generate the community called for by the painting—is pointed to or indicated by the angel's finger: the relation opening between the baby Jesus and the baby John, the foreign element to the holy family now welcomed into the new realm opened by the angelic cut. This welcoming is achieved thanks to the child's blessing gesture, which transmits to John the specific power of grounding over the abyss, thus the new opening to the world as landscape. We, shadowy, exiled foreigners who occupy the abyssal outside of the painting, are called to participate in this communicative trajectory: the angel faces us and draws us in, with the means of its finger directing us toward the figure with whom we are supposed to share a similarity or a commonality, John.

As we have seen, the blessing of the child is that which is enabled by the arrival of the angel as a transcendental valve,[8] thus as something actual that nevertheless allows for the opening to the infinity of the landscape, thereby mitigating the horror of the abyss opening out of the gap between mother and child. Therein lies the redeeming power of the blessing: it is the blessing of the world, the blessing of being allowed, with the mediation of the angel, to open to the world without completely disappearing. It is the power of the child's imagination, of the child as receptor of the angelic image, to be the source of the blessing of the world. The communication of this blessing, which we can understand as an angelic exchange—that which allows for the angelic image to be transmitted or shared—is the essence of play between children, exemplified here in the gestural exchange between

Jesus and John. The function of their (poetic) gestures is not to signify this or that thing in the world or to comprise a specific communication of any content but simply to be the angelic communication of the world. The angel (image) is what the children, between whom a new kind of communication opens, play with. It is through their play—the communication and sharing of an angel, a communication that allows those who occupy the abyssal shadows to be introduced into the world as an inhabited and habitable realm rather than a deserted land of shadows or an enclosed and protected garden—that the darkly abyssal message of the angel with which we opened is transformed into a new experience of the sharing of existence.

In sum, Leonardo's angel marks a crucial and complex transformation in the thinking of the image and in the conception of its place in human life, as well as in the manner of its practice. The angelic image is no longer a figure mediating between this world and another but is a figure standing at the threshold of this world understood as landscape—which is also at the threshold of the world we usually call modern. The modern world stretches between an indeterminate infinity, or a withdrawal from any determination, a withdrawal in relation to which we suffer a disappearance, and a determinate finite realm to which such disappearance and withdrawal are the conditions of opening. The angel, or the image, is both that through which we are exposed to the world *as* infinite landscape and that with the means of which we can come to *inhabit* the landscape, and thus become appropriated to the world, finding our place in it. The angel is, in this sense, a threshold of the world as habitable, as *our* world, precisely because, paradoxically, it is that which is always, and infinitely so, beyond us.

Chapter Two

The Death of God and the
Coming Community (*The Last Supper*)

One of the most famously enigmatic of modern Western images, that is, images
created in the wake of the European Renaissance, Leonardo's *Last Supper* (fig.
2.1) has received attention time and again as a paradigmatic articulation of
the problem of painting as it emerged following the Middle Ages. It occupies
a key moment in the transformation that sacred images underwent in order
to *become* painting, which if we want to grasp what is at stake in modern
painting and modernity more generally (at least from the perspective of art),
we need to understand.[1] The question concerns not just what kinds of images
are created in the new era but what place they occupy in the general economy
of human life—a place that can no longer be defined in terms of establishing
communication with the Christian divine. Of course, I would not claim to
be able to provide an answer in full, but the following discussion wagers that
examining painting as articulated in Leonardo's *Last Supper*, in particular the
source of the work's enigmatic nature, affords insight into the bigger picture
of modern painting and modernity itself, within which images aim to occupy
a position as fundamental as the one they did in the Christian era.

The questions of interest here are not exactly art historical, at least not
in the sense of a specific academic discipline. Rather, they aim to account
for the place of images in human life and the historical transformations this
locus underwent, a process that remains under way. The approach qualifies as
philosophical, provided we understand philosophical questions as concerning
the *whole of existence*. For want of a better term, we may call these questions
artistic-existential. The dimension of Art (a general term covering a range of
images, visual, auditory, written, embodied, etc.) opens at the moment that

35

Figure 2.1. Leonardo, *The Last Supper*. *Source*: Wikimedia Commons, CC public domain.

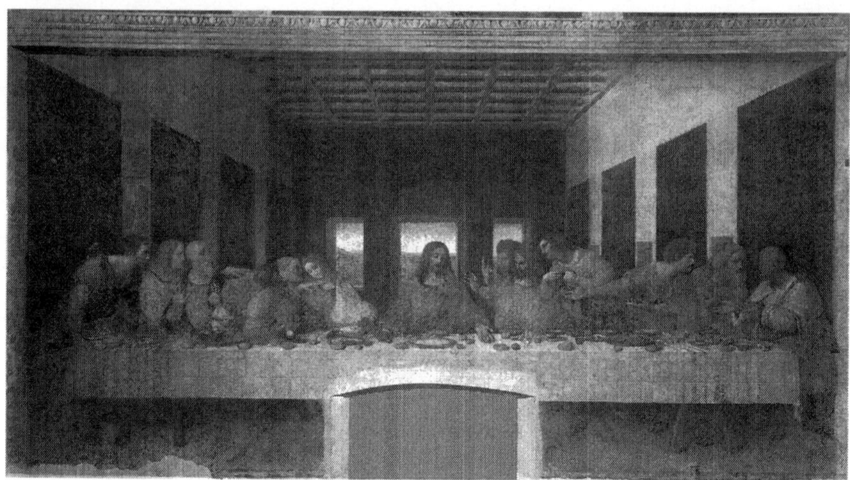

sacred images become transformed into something new (the nature of which we are still far from understanding[2]), and the dimension of Existence is increasingly the name for the Whole in which we find ourselves, when this whole is no longer conceived metaphysically or in terms of a divinely guided cosmos.

Let us then examine what is at stake in the enigma of *The Last Supper* and how the transition into modernity is inscribed in it. The intuition guiding the following (and the book as a whole) is that the being of the enigma—which Leonardo has come preeminently to stand for, in life no less than art[3]—is a cipher of modernity itself and of the place that images take, or at least aim to take, in modernity. If, as has been claimed, medieval sacred images revolve around Christian *mystery* and serve as sites in which the hidden Deity, guide and creator of the world, inscribes itself in earthly materials, modern artistic images orbit another center of gravity, the enigma, which we can tentatively understand as the trace of a withdrawal that points to a beyond (and we can think of the most famous gesture of pointing in Leonardo, that of his *St John the Baptist*) which is not substantial, an immanent beyond we have associated with the concept of the medium.[4]

It is important not to view the enigma as a psychological trait specific to Leonardo. Instead, it represents the focal point of a new way of being in the world, a new way of experiencing and occupying one's place in it. Leonardo is among the first to have grasped, intuitively if not conceptually, that the dimension of a new kind of image is a site for the manifestation and activation of the enigma and, by extension, for maintaining and opening the new way of being for which the enigma (the inscription of the medium) is the focal point. My argument is not that Leonardo's paintings are enigmatic, which has been pronounced many times before, but that his paintings seek, like laboratories for forging a modern way of imaging, to make the enigma "visible" (not only in the sense of becoming an unprecedented object of perception but in the sense of coming to structure an artistic space that draws our gaze in a new way) and, indeed, to transform the enigma into the medium of our existence, through which and by means of which we open up *to* the world. The modern work of art does not exist simply for itself, autonomously (even if one of its fundamental characteristics is the way it enigmatically keeps itself to itself, withdrawn from the world, in the manner of Leonardo's image of an embryo, see figure 2.2), but serves as a kind of embryonic medium to the world,[5] in a sense we will explore in detail.

Figure 2.2. Leonardo, study of foetus in the womb. *Source*: Wikimedia Commons, CC public domain.

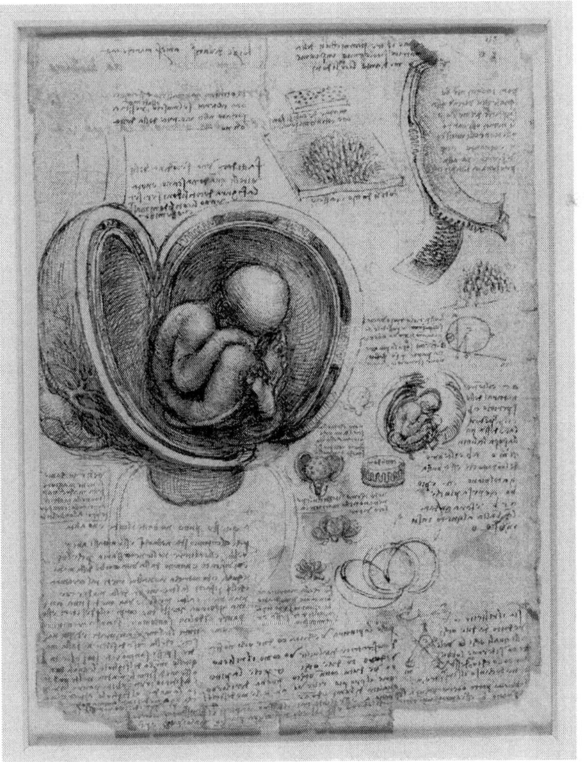

What then is the source of *The Last Supper*'s enigmatic nature, and how are we to start deciphering the work, or even the logic, of the enigma in it? The key, I suggest, lies in the relations the painting establishes between a general sense of unmooring anxiety, expressed through the treatment of the apostles, and the strange sense of detached and passive withdrawal, which paradoxically centralizes and guides our view, in the depiction of Christ. These relations are fundamental to Leonardo's art in general. An intertwinement of unmooring anxiety and guiding or orienting detachment or passive withdrawal lies at the heart of the enigma.

Let us now move closer to *The Last Supper* and see how these issues are developed by it.

Towering above us and pulling our gaze upward, as if on an elevated stage, stands a group of highly animated, larger-than-life figures gathered around a table covered in a blank cloth. Initially, the beholder is carried away by the general animation. A sense of *displacement* prevails: departure from, and possibly the loss of, any assigned or determinate order (a seating arrangement[6]). In consequence of the figures' disordered liveliness, we ourselves lose a sense of place vis-à-vis the painting, a place the painting might otherwise have ordered us into. This dramatic loss of place and the movement that sweeps us along has nothing of the character of revolutionary enthusiasm, or shared and unifying motion, whereby all the participants would join in marching toward some communal future, the promise of a new order. Rather than move in the same direction, the figures are gathered in groups of three, at different centers of activity. As a result, our own animation is subjected to a split corresponding to these competing centers of attention and develops an inner tension; the various groups we are invited to join do not appear to share in a common cause. In addition, tension—if not the possibility of rupture—develops between us and anyone else who might be sharing the space of contemplating the painting with us. For it is by the nature of the divided attention the painting demands that various splits can be introduced among all the beholders, thus preventing them from sharing a common experience, from establishing a community. It is significant that a painting or a fresco in a church—in fact, in a common dining room (*The Last Supper* is located in the refectory of the monastery Santa Maria delle Grazie), thus at the heart of what is supposed to be the experience of a Christian community—harbors, at least as one of its elements, a split or division in shared experience.

But no split can exist without reference to some kind of unity, a whole that is ruptured. Splitting implies rivalry among elements laying claim to represent the One or wield its power—as in, for example, a fight over an inheritance or a struggle for political sovereignty.[7] In this light, we might want to distinguish between dispersal and division, or more precisely dramatic split. Dispersal involves the emergence of multiplicity, with parts no longer under the power of the unifying whole but without the development of a competition or rivalry. A dramatic split, in contrast, implies that the question of unity persists, but the law and order grounding it has been lost or dissolved; here, each element that has been set free (or abandoned) advances a claim to take the place of unity, and the result is tension between them. We might say the split is especially dramatic when it involves a struggle between equal claims at the moment that the common ground is dissolving, as in the disputes between Catholics and Protestants in early modern Europe (or in the contests for power in the theater of the age, e.g., *King Lear*).

It has often been remarked that *The Last Supper* introduces a unique dramatic or theatrical quality into painting.[8] Dramatic unity can be understood, to begin with, as indicating a *common void,* that is, a loss of ground to which each of the elements set free, or loose, still relates: a vacated point of reference they have in common and in relation to which they enter into rivalry. Such rivalries can consist, for example, of each rivalrous party laying claim to being the one able to replace the lost unity, or by having each propose different versions of what a new unifying ground might look like.

At least initially, the various groups into which *The Last Supper* is divided resemble a split more than a dispersal. They share a center, Christ, toward which the figures either gesture or direct their gazes. Yet a true split requires that the point of reference each party has in common is a void, an evacuation of the unifying ground of power, of what we might also call the center of orientation. So is the figure of Christ here—a figure that seems very much present, indeed even august and monumental, being larger in scale than all the others—a common void? Indeed, and in several ways.

To begin with, commentators usually agree that the scene depicts the moment at which Christ announces that one of his closest followers will betray him. The declaration voids the unifying power of a grounding center of orientation—Christ before the announcement, thus Christ as the sovereign center of the group of supposedly unified disciples—in two senses. First, betrayal is a decentering beheading, the dissolution of a center's unifying power. At the moment of betrayal, the center is no longer itself. In consequence, Christ as depicted occupies a center stripped of its power to unify; as we will see, this hollowing out *is* his announcement, or is at its heart. Second, the announcement that *one* of the disciples will betray him without the party in question being identified casts a dissolving shadow over the entire social fabric and the law and order governing the group.[9] Each disciple now stands under the suspicion of being the traitor, and everyone starts suspecting all the others. Christ's declaration voids the social contract, and each disciple loses his secure position in the common order, which has been reduced to a common paranoia.

Now each of the figures is wearing a mask, as it were: he is both himself and a potentially traitorous double. A fissure between seeming and being has cracked open, transforming the world into a *theatrum mundi*, where everyone is an actor on a stage, presenting false identities in an arena of make-believe. In other words, splitting into groups expresses a general ambience of mistrust—Iago has infiltrated the common realm, reducing it to a paranoid theater.

Christ is a void in another, more mysterious and profound way that paradoxically involves his larger-than-life depiction, the fact that he has been painted, if only barely noticeably so, on a different scale than his disciples. This ambiguous suspension of Christ—due to his subtly different scale—between belonging and not belonging to the group is one of Leonardo's major inventions in the painting, with enormous conceptual consequences. The artist does not paint Christ in the realist manner of his forebears, whose works (whether treating the Last Supper or other themes) present all members of the group, including Christ, according to the same dimensions. Nor does he paint him in the medieval way, with a markedly different stature signifying Christ's belonging to a hierarchically higher realm than the rest of the figures.[10] Leonardo's Christ here does not belong to another world, but he is not simply part of the realistically depicted world, either. Rather, Christ both belongs and does not belong to the world; he is part of it and apart from it at the same time.[11] An essential aspect of the painting's enigma derives from the challenge of understanding this contradictory state of belonging and not belonging, a simultaneity that obviously characterizes the duality of the Christ of tradition but which Leonardo reinterprets and displaces.

The issue does not concern the mystery of Christ being simultaneously divine and earthly, as per tradition, but involves a configuration with a different logic, that of what I call the modern Image. Christ is an Image or even, I would argue, a proposition of a modern (or at least other than traditionally theological[12]) approach to the question of the Image. In order to evaluate what is at stake, we need to understand how Leonardo reinterprets the two terms *Christ* and *the Image*—terms that were traditionally connected—through each other. We will keep returning to this question, but for the moment the point to note is how Christ occupies a common void around which all the other figures circulate: being simultaneously a part of the realistically depicted group of apostles and standing apart from them—that is, not fully belonging—Christ is in a sense already gone, or absent, as a fully actual member of the world of his disciples.

The loss of Christ, or his absence from the apostles' world, is not just any loss, for it represents the loss of their center, and the loss of the principle that orders and governs the world. In terms of traditional categories and logic, it can be understood as the loss of the father, that is, the paternal principle whose task it is to order and unify the *entirety* of existence. Yet at the same time Christ is not altogether lost; if so, we would confront a total void in the place he once occupied. Rather, he seems to have returned in some regard, since he still stands among his followers, if in an enlarged and strangely detached manner. This return from loss is at the heart of his enigma, and that of the painting as well. For what does he return *as*? He returns as something I would call an Image. To propose an initial definition, *the Image is a return from loss in which the loss has not been overcome (otherwise we would say that the thing itself has returned as it was) but remains inscribed in what has returned.*

We can begin to see, then, that the loss animating the question of the Image concerns no one thing in particular so much as a relationship. In this case, it means the loss of a paternal Christ as a sovereign center around which the world of the apostles was organized, that gave the apostles their place in an ordering of the world.[13] The Image is what returns out of the loss of the father. Like Eurydice—or any number of other mythical figures associated with passage to the underworld and back—it appears out of the abyss that opened with the loss of the world, a loss that remains inscribed in it. This return means that the Image, in which this loss is inscribed, takes on a spectral character; a kind of ghost, it is marked by restlessness and *atopia*.

So to return to the question: what does Christ return *as* in Leonardo's painting, or even more precisely, what kind of Image does he return as? Possibilities are multiple here. He might have come back as nothing but a memory (and memory itself can be defined as an image emerging out of loss and absence, to which the apostles are attached in mourning and, probably, guilt). Or he might be a memory transformed along Freudian lines into an idealized image by attempts to cover over this guilt: the slain primal father returning as a god to the sons responsible for his death. Such an idealized image results from the transformation of the Image—that return from the loss of the center of the world, and in which the inscribed loss implies a no longer fully belonging to the world—into something that has a supernatural status beyond anything within the world and henceforth serves as guide to those left behind. Or it might be that Christ here is a hallucinatory image, one that marks the loss of the father figure as a traumatic one defying conscious grasp, a kind of a repetitive haunting, an image erupting out of the apostles' common nightmare. Finally, a deeper possibility exists: Christ comes back as a new type of Image that functions not just as a memory, an idealized transfiguration, or a repetitive traumatic haunting, but as a new way of understanding the relations between death and life, or as that *through which* our experience of death and life will be transformed.

These options are not exhaustive,[14] and they are all probably operative simultaneously in Leonardo's painting (although to me the last option, which points to the artist's most profound achievement, is the most dominant). Whatever the case, we can say that Christ, at once standing apart from and standing among the apostles, is the one who has departed as actual center (thus as father) and returned as an Image, an Image in which is inscribed (much like Hamlet's ghost returning after his death as paternal center of the kingdom[15]) the trace of his departure.[16]

The Appearance of Withdrawal

At the heart of *The Last Supper*, then, both at its literal center and at the center of the question it poses for us, is the emergence of Christ as an Image, a ghostly figure of return inscribing, to begin with, the loss of the world. This loss is expressed in the anxiety and commotion of the apostles, anxiety being the affect attached to the loss of the ordering unification of one's world and the exposure to the voiding of that which grounded it.

The essential relation between Christ and the Image had already been established by theological tradition, especially in the writings of Paul and Augustine. Inasmuch as his painting is not only an image *of* Christ but shows Christ *as* an Image (and also the Image *as a* Christ, i.e., the Image as a redeemer of the world, a topic to which we will return), Leonardo does the same. However, Leonardo's *pictorial* interpretation of Christ as Image cannot be subsumed under the theological interpretation of Christ. Instead, the painting aims to become a new source of authority that exceeds the theology with which it is in conversation.

Our guiding question is therefore the following: if Christ is indeed an Image, a claim already put forward by the Christian theological tradition, or perhaps something we can view as a paradigmatic occurrence of an Image-event, can an activity dedicated to making an Image happen—namely, painting—have something to say about Christ and about the Image that exceeds the theological tradition and in fact enters into a rivalry with it? In other words, we might want to reverse the usual analysis and open the question of the meaning of Christ (the one who dies and comes back, and who is an Image) from the point of view of the work of the pictorial image rather than the other way around, which is to open the question of the pictorial image from the point of view of Christ, as interpreted within the theological tradition. The matter concerns artists from Leonardo and Bruegel to Chaplin and Pasolini, and likely others before and after.

To say that theology and painting (and art in general) enter into a rivalry over the question of the interpretation of the Image/Christ implies that the Image precedes and exceeds them both, that it represents an enigmatic event around which they are constructed and which they attempt, by separate means, to capture (in the sense of Orson Welles's famous definition of the task of art, as trying to capture "lightning in a bottle"). The challenge that painting poses to theology may have always implicitly existed, but it is with, and as, Renaissance or modern painting (and attendant theoretical discourses) that this challenge comes to the fore. Henceforth, the opening of such a rivalry over the Image means that the dimension of the Image is liberated into its own enigma, allowing this enigma to start speaking beyond its theological interpretation, to flash however illusively in its own light, even if it might turn out that any attempt to behold it in full and seize it fast—like Orpheus's attempt to behold Eurydice at the moment between death and life, departure and return—ends up with nothing at all, or even with one's own dismemberment.

It might be said that in linking its foundational event, Christ, together with the concept of the Image, Christian theology allowed the enigma of the Image to shine forth in its absolute *centrality* (and at the same time permitted the mystery at the heart of religion, as never before, to be fully illuminated by the mystery of the Image, perhaps even to be understood *as* such mystery). However, theology immediately harnessed this splendor of the image and subjected it to its own concerns. For its part, perhaps the most profound significance of Renaissance painting is the challenge it posed to Christian theology regarding the Image, at once preserving the centrality of the mystery, or enigma, of the Image and liberating the image from the hermeneutic grasp of theology. In the context of the West, there is thus perhaps no centralization of the question of the Image without Christianity and Christian theology, and no liberation of this centralization, no access to the question of the Image *as such*, without Renaissance painting. It is through the figure of Christ, in his relation to the question of painting, that this enormous drama has to pass, and it is in *The Last Supper*, possibly the most paradigmatic modern (or Renaissance onward) figuration of Christ, that the drama becomes fully visible.

Let us look more closely then at the pictorial context within which Christ appears as an Image, or better yet within which he *is* an Image. What is the pictorial task vis-à-vis the question of the Image, a question that precedes and exceeds painting, just as it precedes and exceeds theology, and to which these two "discourses" propose different answers?

Opening onto the Landscape

We can start by examining the way Christ functions in terms of how Leonardo's painting orchestrates the adventure of our *eye movement*, of our way of *looking*. We have already remarked that in front of *The Last Supper*, our gaze is dispersed, split between different centers of attention (the groups of the apostles) that are in tension with one another. At the same time, our eyes are drawn to the central figure, to which all the other figures in the painting refer by look or gesture. Leonardo's work establishes a rhythm of being scattered in anxiety and calmed by a center the function of which is to serve as the solution to this anxiety. However, we have also seen that the center of the painting, which is occupied by Christ, is in a complex way a central void. Thus, it is a paradoxical center, a center of a new kind, one that marks the absence of a (traditional) center, understood as a present point of reference in relation to which everything else can gather, and from the ordering power of which it receives its unity—in traditional terms, a father. Our gaze does not find an instance of authority under the dominion and ordering power of which it is guided but instead meets a strange void.

However—and this turn of events is crucial—the center that the eyes reach in Christ, which proves to be a void, provides the occasion for our eyes *to begin to move in a new direction*. This direction opens (onto) the landscape. Christ is positioned in such a way that our eyes are immediately drawn to look behind, or beyond, him, through the windows and toward an expanse characterized, like all of Leonardo's landscapes, by *sfumato*[17]: the effacement of contours through gradations that blur determinate formal limits and, depriving the eye of any stopping point, draw it onward into a sort of infinity, an unending movement.

The function of the center is transformed by its becoming a central void. *The center no longer serves to subject us to an order but exposes us to an infinity—and to the freedom of infinity—by withdrawing, or voiding, any determined order.* At the same time, however, this voidance is not a chaotic dispersal but a new kind of centralizing guidance. That is, the central void is no longer to be understood purely in negative terms, as standing for a loss of authority and ordering power; instead, it should be thought of as the positively valorized site where a new kind of eye and a new mode of looking emerge. The center, then, is transformed into a void out of which, or by means of which, we open our eyes: the center-void is a new *medium* of vision, through which we see. Mediated by the new center-void, our eyes now see *through*, or *by means of*, the loss of a paternal center that organizes the whole—thus the loss of any determined coordinates that order the eyes. The one whose medium is the center-void, figured here as Christ, comes to inhabit a new realm, that of the world as infinite landscape, thus a realm with no stable point of origin or end. Leonardo's Christ, in other words, is the medium of the world as landscape. Leonardo's Christ, then, not only stands for the dissolution of the metaphysical ground but also comes to serve as a new ground himself, a new power of grounding, to whom we constantly need to return as the originary source for the disclosure of the non-metaphysical world. In other words, Christ is, paradoxically, a *grounding abyss*, a source of a world without a stable center of reference.

It is this originary power that marks the distinction between the image in general and the Image that is (a) Christ. The former can be defined as a ghostly return flashing at the enigmatic moment that we lose paternal anchoring in the world, when we are exposed to a constitutive ground-lessness—whether as the irruption of a repressed memory (a memory that carried an excess that could not be integrated into the world); the trace of a traumatic encounter; a miraculous, angelic, or erotic event (the arrival of something out of nowhere recognizable in the causally structured world); or in other ways. An image transforms into an *Image as a Christ*—and this is the task of the painter as Leonardo develops it here—when the enigmatic moment of loss that the image occupies becomes the birthplace of a new medium, through which we open to the world as the infinity of the landscape. Allegorically speaking, Leonardo shows that at its core every painting has the task of transforming the image (an excess that signaled the loss of world to the extent that it could not be integrated into the world, but which *returned* as indicating the unrelenting restlessness of that which cannot be integrated yet also cannot be eliminated) into *a* Christ, an event of redemption: serving as the origin of the world, giving us the world at the very moment of its birth—to which we repeatedly need to return as the source and resource of our life.

The Last Supper comes to function as the site of an eternal return. The painting is that to whose centralizing power we need to return time and again in order to open to the landscape, and be dispersed, only to return to the center again, the source and resource of the landscape. In our encounter with the painting, then, our eyes are drawn in, only to wander among the scattered apostles; then, in a further turn, our gaze is pulled back to Christ, the center of gravity as it were, before it proceeds to the landscape into which he provides a portal, a trajectory we need to undergo over and over. The continuous, recurring movement introduces us to a new way of inhabiting a world with no center, a world without beginning or end.

We can thus understand the initial movement of our eyes, from the anxious dispersal of the apostles to the void that is Christ, as belonging to the moment of the dissolution of a metaphysically organized world. In this moment, the loss of a grounding center has left us in frantic disarray, and we might be seeking to restore the center, only to discover a void (much like Hamlet's desperate and failed attempt to restore the father whose ghostly void he has encountered). Yet this void proves to be transformative, becoming the medium of a new world that lacks a centering ground. Or rather, it becomes the medium of a world whose centering ground is the abyss as a lack of ground, yet which opens onto the landscape. In this sense, as our gaze returns to the apostles following the transformative encounter with Christ the center-void, we no longer experience them in a state of anxiety. Instead, they display a new kind of dispersal, the dispersal of those who have come, through the medium of Christ the Image, to inhabit a landscape: a realm whose only grounding center is the transformative abyss of ground, and in which each of the inhabitants is not subjected to a pregiven unifying power but is rather one locus among others in an open infinity that can be understood as being in constant creation. This constant creation opens its inhabitants to each other over and over with no pregiven grounding and ordering plan. The dislocation of the apostles should be understood no longer as the result of a loss of metaphysical unifying center to be regained (i.e., as a dramatic struggle) but as the expression of the fact that the world is at heart a creative dispersal. What unifies and grounds this realm is, paradoxically, the fact that there is no stable foundation but only *a creative power*, expressed though Christ the center-void, of opening. It is this discovery, following the transformative encounter with Christ, that the apostles, and we in concert with them, now need to become the messengers of. Each apostle, each of us, now comes to function as a locus in a world without center, a landscape in constant transformation and reopening.

In affective terms, we have transitioned from an anxious loss of the metaphysically structured world into what we can call groundless creativity. Taking Christ-the-Image as our new medium, we participate in the creation of the world, its constantly renewed opening as landscape. *Beyond anxiety, we are called, through the Image as a Christ, into the world as landscape in whose creation we participate or co-create.* The calming, enigmatic affect of the withdrawn Christ is that affect beyond anxiety at the heart of the creative, eternal reopening of the world as landscape. Beyond anxiety lies resurrection, a ceaselessly renewed world without beginning or end, a world of eternal movement, of unceasing creative dispersal. Our affective transformation occurs in our passage from a theater of paranoia—a realm where the dissolution of the centralizing paternal power casts a shadow, a darkness effacing identity that inflicts a split between seeming and being—into a resurrected realm liberated from paranoia.

This realm harbors what Eve Sedgwick has called "reparative" affects in distinction to paranoid ones. They include love, which we can understand as creative disclosure enabled by the call of the voiding power. The paranoid split that defines the theatrical world stems from the "shadow" cast by paternal loss, the loss of unifying ground. Inhabitants of this world are corroded by a loss experienced as effacement of identity inasmuch as their assigned place vanishes. They are struck by a void, as it were, disconnected from the ground of their existence. Yet there is a strange sort of negative presence to this void, one that can come to function as a mask, something that covers identity and which starts to serve as a site for the creation of various *false* identities, identities that serve to hide the lack, or loss, of being (i.e., the loss of being connected to the source that grants being, the father as metaphysical grounding in a pre-given ordered world) characterizing their now shadowy existence. What we can call the "world of resurrection," the eternal return of infinite creation through an Image-as-a-Christ, transforms the absence arising from the disappearance of the paternal center and turns it into a *creative void* (which should be distinguished from the mask as a place for the forging of false identities). This creative void is now the medium through which we open to a landscape, a world in constant transformation, whose elements are guided not by any centralizing metaphysical ground. In the resurrected world, then, the shadow of the paternal disappearance is no longer a void or lack of being onto which the possibility of the mask is projected, but a *voiding* creativity that removes the metaphysical ground from us in order to open us to the landscape. The masked Iago is transformed into a voiding Christ.[18]

Let us think a bit more closely about this remarkable moment of the emergence of a new kind of center, a center-void, which serves as a new kind of medium of seeing, one that opens upon a landscape. If this void, the site of the happening of the Image, merits the name "center" it is not only with respect to its occupation of the middle of the painting but also for its power in orchestrating our vision, our manner of looking. It is the center of vision, in other words, not as a spatial *object* but as its *medium*, the medium of vision.

It has often been remarked that, in modern painting, the activity of looking itself becomes the subject matter: by means of the work of art, the eye can come to "see" itself, or experience itself, looking. This observation is not wrong, but it is incomplete, given the more complex "picture" of looking developed by Leonardo here. For it is not that, in starting to open to the landscape in *The Last Supper* with the means of the center-void, the eye simply experiences itself looking instead of only seeing objects, as if the capacity to look were a secure property of the eyes or of the one who looks, a property that painting enables us to access. The eye does not look, or does not open into looking, out of its own powers, so to speak, but is *called* to look, even forced into looking, by being introduced into a realm, the landscape, that voids determinate relations, the standing order of things, which the one who is forced to look might have been said to occupy. To look is to be called to open to a realm emptied of any predetermined relations and ordering of things. The (human) eyes have a void at, or as, their center, which means they are subjected to the call of the landscape. It is in this sense that *the landscape is the center of the eyes*, that which calls them into looking. This center is "outside" and "inside" at once—external and internal to the eyes, extimate to them, in Lacan's vital phrasing. It is external in the sense that the eye does not precede the landscape; rather, the landscape precedes the eye, the landscape being the world-as-infinity, thus a realm of relations with no determined and pregiven order in the midst of which the eyes, or the one who looks, finds themselves *in medias res*. And it is internal in the sense that it is the very being of the landscape *as* landscape, the infinity of the world, its lack of predetermination, which the eye, or the one who looks, is called by (rather than being called by any specific "object" in, or component of, this infinite world or landscape) and that as such makes the eye the unique and mysterious thing that it is. The Image (as a Christ) occupies this extimate moment between eye and landscape; it is the way the landscape comes to inhabit the eye as its centralizing call, calling it to See.

Fundamentally, the question of the relations among the dispersed apostles, understood now as those who inhabit a world newly conceived as landscape, is that of *community*: occupying a realm that is shared. We can picture the world understood as landscape as a common realm that exposes everything and everyone who inhabits it to each other with no preordained order, thus without hierarchy, and we can think of this common exposure as a *communication*. Such communication does not belong to the human, nor does it originate with the human or with any specific type of the landscape's occupants. Rather, it is that into which human being is "inserted" and in which it takes part as one among many, all of which are equal. At the same time, human participation in the communication, the common exposure, of the world or landscape proves exceptional because the core of the human (what used to be called its "essence") is empty—that is, it is open and with no predetermined terms. While every other exposed member of the landscape seems to be determined by the type of relations it can establish within the common realm, the human does not seem to be determined in the same manner but is characterized as the one who can unpredictably form ever-new sets of relations within the common. In other words, the human is not just another occupant of the landscape, not just one of the members in a general communication, but *is* itself a landscape, or more precisely is the one inhabited by the landscape as such, understood as infinitely open common exposure. *The exceptionality of the human consists of being a part of the landscape that also reflects the landscape as such, or communication as such. The human is the ex-posed communicator.* The essence of the human is communication (the sharing of the landscape) as such, as infinitely open and undetermined, and in this sense the fundamental human question is that of community, the relation among those whose occupation of the common can never be determined in advance. However, human beings do not "possess" communication, or *language*, but receive it from the world or landscape (understood as the immanent beyond of medium), and receive it as something they can never will or determine since it does not originate in them—and to will is to be an origin—but can only witness, we might say, that is, receive passively while opening to what they receive.

The moment of the Image, understood as the moment of being inflicted with the call of the landscape, is the advent of the shocking reception of an originary communication—that is, the landscape/language/ the announcement of the common world (the exposure of everything in the world to each other without predetermination)—that one cannot will but only passively, hence shockingly, receive, from outside oneself in the manner of a reluctant prophet.

What we have called the new center, the medium of the eyes, can therefore be understood as a fundamental or constitutive ex-centricity, and this in two ways. First, the center-void is ex-centric in the sense that it functions as a call to the eyes from outside, or even beyond (in the sense of beyond any actual thing, what philosophers have named the absolute outside), from the world or landscape (understood as groundless medium of communication). Moreover, the center-void is ex-centric in that it indicates that the world or landscape does not *have* a center, in the sense of a core point of reference around which unity coalesces, but is a temporal-spatial dispersal in which any one place is equal to any other: all sites share equally in a communication that does not originate in any of them but occurs among all of them because of their equal exposure to one another. The center-void, then, is an ex-centricity that nevertheless constitutes our very essence, inhabiting us most intimately, making us who we are. It is the intimate ex-centricity of the world/landscape whose shock the irruption of the Image (that which surges forth out of the collapse of the metaphysical center) registers and effects.

In this light, the "center" of the world is revealed as being nothing but communication, the communication of everything with everything else, without a central point of reference serving to ground it all. This is the reason for which God has often been said to be nowhere and everywhere.[19] God, or the divine, is nothing other than the communication of the world as such, of everything with everything, rather than any specific grounding substance or law, a communication of which the human is an exceptional witness. This communication is something we witness, that is, something we receive despite our will, as well as something we share with each other, a sharing that is the essence of our being as linguistic beings but does not derive from us and is not our property or power. The Image-Christ is the *appearance* of this communicative medium, both in the sense that it is that through which communication arrives, through which we open to the call of communication, shockingly receiving the world as landscape, and in the sense that it is the exceptional, paradoxical appearance, the mysterious coming to shine, of that which in a way does not appear, the void at the heart of appearance. This void, this nonappearance or invisibility, is nothing but communication/language as such, which itself does not appear, by virtue of the fact that it is what we can call the *medium* of appearance, that with the means of which all things appear, that is, appear as part of universal communication of everything with everything. To appear means to become a moment in an open question of communication (an openness that itself is not a part of that which takes place *in* the open), the question of how what appears stands in relation to everything else, how it shares with everything else a common realm. Christ, as shining appearance of the void, is then the appearance of communication, or the paradoxical appearance of the medium of appearance, a medium that is in excess over every specific thing that appears in it. Another way of putting it is that Leonardo's Christ/the Image is, in the terms of the Introduction to this book, the empty threshold of or to appearance (empty in the sense of not being any specific appearing thing). In the words of Pascal, which we can now inflect slightly differently in light of the above: "There is a God-shaped *vacuum* in the heart of each man (i.e., in our terms the void of communication) which cannot be satisfied by any created thing but only by God the Creator, made known (i.e., coming to shine as an Image) through Jesus Christ."[20]

Painting, then, at least in the transformation it undergoes with Leonardo, allows for the advent of the Image qua *a* Christ, through which we receive the gift of the world, and in this regard painting can be said to redeem the world in the sense of bringing it about, allowing us to inhabit it as a landscape rather than a metaphysical realm dominated by a grounding center. Like human being itself, painting appears *in* the world, or in the landscape, not (only) as a simple occupier of the world but in the capacity of voiding it of any centralizing reference point, and allowing us to open to it as being a landscape, the infinite communication of everything with everything, or language.

At the origin of language is, perhaps paradoxically, an Image, the shocking event with the means of the shining of which we are exposed to ex-centric communication beyond our grasp. We can understand this shocking moment of exposure in relation to another fundamental, "linguistic" aspect of painting: its muteness. A painting is, as is often pointed out, mute, yet we need to understand the significance of this muteness within the context of the question of the emergence of the Image as we have presented it. What is muteness in this context? It is both the painting's silence and our own loss of words—our being devoid of speech—in the presence of the painting: like the apostles who have lost their ordered place, we find our capacity to say and articulate what we see as lacking, taken out as we are of any recognizable order of relations. The encounter with the center-void, understood now as intimate ex-centricity, means that the center of speaking and gazing is neither *in* the subject nor lies in a willing authority outside the subject, determining the subject from without. The center, the *origin* of speaking and looking, in the sense of being the medium enabling or originating them, is simultaneously inside and outside; it strikes the subject, at the moment of the Image, with the gift of speech as the shocking arrival of the world as the infinity of communication beyond and before personal will, and which is thus experienced as an originary muteness, an originary incapacity to will speech and be its determining origin.

One of the interpretative enigmas of *The Last Supper* involves determining the content of Christ's speech. It is taken for granted in the critical tradition's discussions of the painting that we are witnessing a moment of his *speech*, yet which moment is unclear. Is it when he announces, "One of you will betray me"? The moment he declares "This is my body," pointing to the bread? Or perhaps some other moment? At any rate, we can say, the most fundamental aspect of Christ's speech here is his *pictorial* silence,[21] his muting Image at the threshold of enunciation, which becomes the heart of a new community (lest we forget, the painting occupied the common dining room of the monastery). A new opening of communication, with which all those who relate to the painting are now gifted, beyond the divisions with each other into which they have initially been thrown upon losing the center. For being gifted, through infliction with muting, with language/the Word, each of the members facing the painting comes to share in the infinite communication of the world (infinity being the transmission occurring between the finite occupants that have the world in common), a communication that decenters each one of them, allowing the only center to be the infinite communication of the world itself, a communication of what has no center in the sense of a grounding point of reference.

By way of the landscape as infinite communication, the apostles accede to what we can understand as the freedom of speech—not in the sense that each one now speaks at will, or becomes the willful origin or center of speech, irrespective of the others, but in the sense that they all share in a language ex-centric to them, the circulating communication of the landscape of which they now form a part, where every point is equal to every other. The freedom of speech (which means a speech opening not in relation to any centralizing authority, not even that of a willful subject) is the opening of a communication without center which we are unable to will but with which we can only be shockingly gifted, from the outside. The muting gift of Christ grants freedom of speech, opening a new community without center, the community of those who share the landscape.

One of the fundamental aspects of Christ-the-Image, and the Image as a Christ (redeeming the world), as one who both belongs and does not belong to the apostles (a group we can now extend to include us, the viewers) is to be understood in relation to this intimate ex-centricity he announces. He is the one who is both outside, thus who does not belong, yet inside, thus belonging most intimately to each member of the new community inflicted with his gifting and shocking muteness qua the origin of (the freedom of) speech. He can be said both to belong and not to belong in the sense that he is the *medium* of looking and of speaking. The medium always belongs and does not belong, for it allows the field of vision and/or language to open while standing beyond any specific position or place. Christ as intimate ex-centricity, or as an *intimate alien*, a new medium of the landscape or world as infinite communication without grounding center, is simultaneously part of, and apart from, the dispersed community whose heart he is.

Chapter Three

Out of the Blue

The Play of the World and the Overcoming of Sacrifice
(*The Virgin and Child with Saint Anne*)

An emissary of the sky, yet holding the grounding power of the earth—light, yet heavy, saintly, yet slightly demonic, unmistakably real yet dreamlike and ideal, erect and firm, yet flowing and soft, earthy, yet ethereal and divine, eternal, yet mortal, traumatizing, yet healing. Strange like a tribal totem or an Easter Island head, mysteriously sacred like a medieval icon, yet at the same time enigmatically modern: This is St Anne, in whom, perhaps more than any other figure by Leonardo, is orchestrated the contradictions and tensions at the heart of the artist's work.

Each of the paintings we have examined include a strange figure who stands for the arrival of an image or functions as the allegory of such arrival, be it the angel in *The Annunciation* and *Virgin of the Rocks* or Christ in *The Last Supper*. Likewise, but to an even subtler and more uncanny effect, *The Virgin and Child with St Anne* (fig. 3.1) presents a somewhat alien figure, St Anne, emerging in a pictorial world that is by and large represented in a realistic mode. In each, a new kind of realism, one we associated with the term *landscape*, and with life in the world, understood *as* landscape, opens, as we have seen. Leonardo shows and explores such realistic realms jointly with an alien figure simultaneously belonging, or immanent, to the world, and not belonging to it, standing *beyond*. While sacred art in the Christian tradition is also dedicated to making otherworldly figures manifest, Leonardo employs the same iconography to another end. Christ, Mary, and the angels no longer mark the arrival of a sacred emissary from a transcendent

Figure 3.1. Leonardo, *The Virgin and Child with Saint Anne. Source*: Wikimedia Commons, CC public domain.

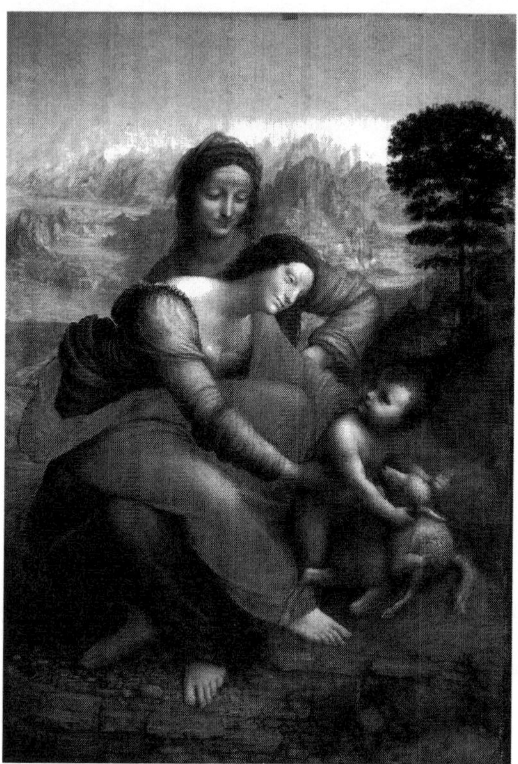

and invisible ontological realm (allowing the painting itself to be viewed as a sacred emissary) so much as they signify foreignness immanent to the world and synonymous with its very possibility.[1]

Accordingly, I have also tried to show that—in contrast to contemporaries fascinated by quattrocento perspectival realism—Leonardo preserves the dimension of foreignness characterizing sacred works. As a result, he insists on a certain ontological difference that cuts through the pictorial world and splits it into two interlaced (rather than substantially distinct, as would have been the logic guiding sacred paintings) levels.[2] This ontological difference, or ontological interlace,[3] is the one between a realist world (realism being understood not as some kind of representational adequacy but as the becoming manifest of a dimension of reality *to* things, whatever that might mean, which we will get to) and the foreignness immanent to it, which cannot be separated from its very possibility.

"Image" refers both to the intrusive dimension of foreignness inscribed in a specific exceptional figure (angel, Christ, St Anne, etc.), and to the painting in its entirety, the latter from two perspectives: first, when the painting in its entirety is conceived on its own (i.e., oblivious to the outside world per se), as a site dedicated to letting this strangeness/the Image, that which belongs and does not belong, appear; and second, when the painting is conceived in relation to the world outside the painting, as a site whose function is to introduce us to the world by serving as the *threshold of the world*. In such case the painting serves as the (maternal, at least in St Anne) *medium* for a new opening of the world, a world characterized as haunted by an immanent strangeness.

The task at hand, then, is to understand this new type of ontological difference, which transforms the ontological division between two realms that guided Christian painting.

Like all of Leonardo's works on Christian themes, the painting is not only structured around a new inscription of ontological difference but allegorizes, and is "about," the transition between the two systems of painting, thus the two modes (medieval and modern) of inscribing ontological difference. We can trace the shift by briefly looking at a traditional treatment of the subject of St Anne, Virgin, and Child. In the painting below, for example, the three figures are orchestrated according to a hieratic and hierarchical order (see Figure 3.2). The vertical, static arrangement indicates an idea of a stable and stabilizing, indeed eternal and changeless, metaphysical structure, from high to low and large to small; it indicates a transcendent realm separate from this world that we can glimpse, as if in a vision, by means of the painting. In ontological terms, the work divides reality into two domains: the invisible, transcendent realm and the earthly, visible realm. St Anne, at the head of the hierarchy, corresponds with the top of the visual frame, as if to show that the hierarchy's true source, God the Father, resides beyond the frame. The invisibility of the father, incorporeal spirituality, is supposed to stand at the source of the nonearthly, virginal mode of succession (Anne was also thought to have given birth to Mary without sin).

By extension, the invisibility beyond the frame is active as an impregnating spiritual force guiding the hierarchy of creation as an unseen law. We, in turn, are its offspring, as it were. Through the painting, which functions as a womb, so to speak, we are spiritually reborn into the invisible law of the father and become members of the holy family. Additionally, perhaps,

Figure 3.2. *St Anna Metterza, Oratorio di San Lorenzo all'alpe Seccio. Source:* Wiki-media Commons, CC public domain.

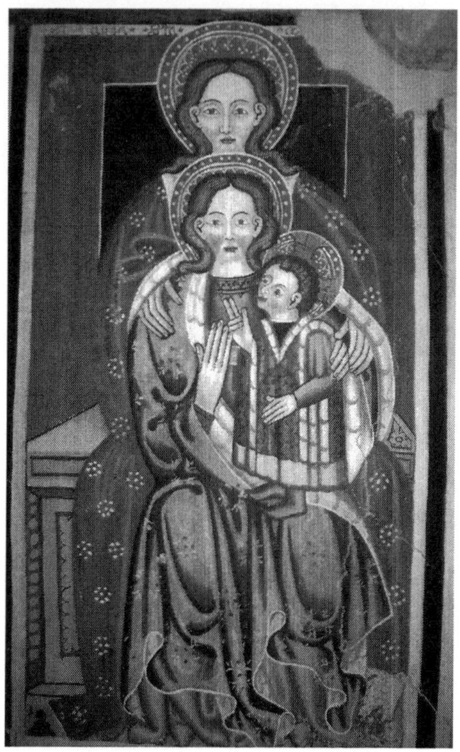

we are called to give imaginative, spiritual birth to new life, to extend the holy family into an ordered Christian community. From this standpoint, the Image-as-virginal, spiritual womb is a matrix for (re)generation that ensures the smooth transition between transcendent spiritual power and the visible world while itself belonging fully to neither.[4] The static, flat image, in its withdrawal from the three or four dimensionality of the material world, signals the miraculous ability to partake, like Christ himself, in both realms.[5]

Leonardo's St Anne reworks this logic and represents a new inscrip-tion of ontological difference. As in *The Last Supper*, the exceptional figure (St Anne), the Image functioning as the center around which the painting revolves, is enigmatically withdrawn, and emerges, so to speak, within the context of an anxious scene of separation and loss (or more precisely a scene of anxiety, love, and desire). Separation and loss here are perhaps even more primordial than is the case for the apostles, separated as they are from Christ the father figure, for they concern a bond between mother and child.

In contrast to art based on structures of narrative succession, where the stream of "information" to which we are exposed is somewhat controlled by the order of segments, painting presents itself in a single simultaneous moment, in its entirety; it cannot dictate the sequence of perceptions to the same degree as can other arts. Consequently, the background mood attending our encounter with a painting is perhaps marked by a greater amount of anxiety than is the case with other arts because the medium itself provides minimal guidance. We cannot say where a painting begins or ends, or where at all it is heading. The basic condition of painting is extreme disorientation, even if it is bound, at the very least, by the basic coordinates of up and down, left and right, and front and back. Painting is not, as per Lessing's famous distinction, a spatial art, or an art of simultaneity, opposed to temporal arts of succession. Rather, the pictorial surface is a potential infinity of invisible, virtual temporal trajectories coexisting simultaneously, which are released by the painting's decontextualized, or cutoff, nature. Not forming part of a worldly continuum, thus not being part any actual sense and direction of things, the cutoff pictorial surface exposes us to every possible direction and sense.

Every actual line and every figure come forth out of this virtual infinity and disorientation, suspended, as it were, between two possibilities. Either they can function in the service of actual or actualized visibility, effacing their point of origin, or they can function in the service of this virtuality, becoming what we can call *messengers* of infinity. In the latter case, the task of painting is to devise ways for visible actuality to arise that, at the same time, shows and activates its invisible and infinite background. By dint of doing so, it allows invisibility to "speak"; the painting permits us to orient ourselves not by erasing the originary disorientation of virtual infinity but in allowing us to be those whose lives are oriented by opening us to its originary disorienting background, now functioning in a new way, as the constant resource, in the manner of Christ of *The Last Supper*, for the reopening of the world. The task, we might say, is to teach us to live (always an actual task) *with* our virtual and invisible "nature," which means being suspended between actual finitude and virtual infinity.

Both the medieval St Anne and Leonardo's figure of the Mother of Mary are meant as messengers of invisibility and of infinity, yet each has a very different conception of what this entails. In the former, invisibility is conceived as a realm separate from the pictorial space and the material world and located over and above them and the world. For Leonardo, however, and for much of the modern pictorial tradition to follow, infinite invisibility is a haunting background *immanent* to the visible realm. Here, infinite invisibility does not belong to another, separate realm but is the unpredictable openness of *this* world, inscribed in each of its inhabitants. The task is to show how the landscape—an unpredictably open realm, where relations are never given in advance—marks its occupants as not fully formed, not fully determined within a set configuration of things but characterized by their exposure to an openness they can neither control nor avoid. Revealing infinity, in this sense, involves showing how trajectories of movement composing the painting never follow a set direction, like the hierarchical top-to-bottom one characterizing the Christian St Anne, but can go any which way, in a manner that defies prediction.

Accordingly, even though every route and trajectory in the painting is actual, we feel it emerging from an inexhaustible background where no predetermined sense of direction is inscribed. Consider, for instance, the drippings and unpredictable lines composing a painting by Jackson Pollock, a paradigmatic case of a modern image in the tradition of Leonardo, which express a democratic and nonhierarchical plurality of directions of movement, their dizzying simultaneity preventing any total grasp of a given direction to the whole (not unlike the way *The Last Supper*'s apostles' simultaneous gestures and movements, which emerge from the loss of a grounding whole, turn them into a democratic plurality of sorts). We can understand these lines as emerging out of an infinite virtuality that retains a haunting presence beyond what is visible. In a sense, the ghostly background itself cannot be exhausted by the visibility of the unpredictable lines emerging from it, but continues to haunt precisely by virtue of its inability to be exhausted. Such haunting becomes "visible" as the inexhaustible excess over and above all the actual trajectories and movements. Each drip or line is, in this sense, a messenger of infinity, or that through which infinite virtuality comes to show. However, Leonardo includes an additional logical element (i.e., an element in the context where the pictorial project is understood as that of the engagement with, and showing of, the whole) in this modern, non-metaphysical task to express infinity: the exceptional figure, as in the angel, Christ, St Anne, and others. It is the exceptional figures that can be understood most fully as messengers of infinity in that they are the ones in whom the openness of infinity as such—characterized by an absolute exteriority, an excess beyond any determined form and trajectory—is inscribed. Whereas every finite member of the infinite world that we have called the landscape bears the mark of infinity, this does not mean they display or show openness *to* it. There must be a specific member of the landscape to serve as the mediator through which infinity becomes, and remains, active in a way that keeps the landscape from being appropriated to a specific directionality and order. This exceptional figure must simultaneously belong and not belong to the finite realm so that, *within* the finite realm, it can be the messenger of an "absolute outside," as Deleuze would put it.[6]

The exceptional figure signals that pictorial space has the task of becoming the arena for the display of a modern infinity, understood as the immanent and unpredictable openness of the world, with no pregiven order or hierarchy. However, the space Leonardo creates is not completely destitute of hierarchy and orientation in the manner of Pollock. Rather, as we started to see in our discussion of *The Last Supper*, it is a space that, on the one hand, dissolves the metaphysically conceived, hierarchical arrangement of medieval painting, opening up an infinite landscape, and on the other hand, orients this space by establishing an exceptional point within it. This exceptional point or figure is not a hierarchical center so much as an energetic core around which, paradoxically, a world without a center revolves, like the eye of a storm or the eddy of a flood, a source of fascination for Leonardo in many of his drawings. For instance, see figure 3.3, which, on its own, can serve as a perfect allegory of the Leonardian transformation of visual space where we leave framed organization—the square opening to the right and out of which the water erupts—with its divisions between inside and outside, center and periphery, etc., and enter a new, circular logic where things do have a sort of orienting center, but this center in not a hierarchical one, but is rather nothing but an originating void around which everything starts to circulate, precisely because there is no positive hierarchical center. In the St Anne painting, the famous swirl in the virgin's clothes on the left side of the painting (when facing us), which Freud seemed to think had the shape of a bird, exhibits the same circular movement, as if showing us in miniature the movement of the painting as a whole. We might note the proximity of this abyssal circulation around the void to two very famous moments in Hitchcock: the abyssally circular lock of hair in the painting of Carlotta in *Vertigo*, the gazing of which evokes Scotty's nightmare scene, and the relation between the evacuated eye and draining water in *Psycho*'s shower scene.

Figure 3.3. Leonardo, study of water. *Source*: Wikimedia Commons, CC public domain.

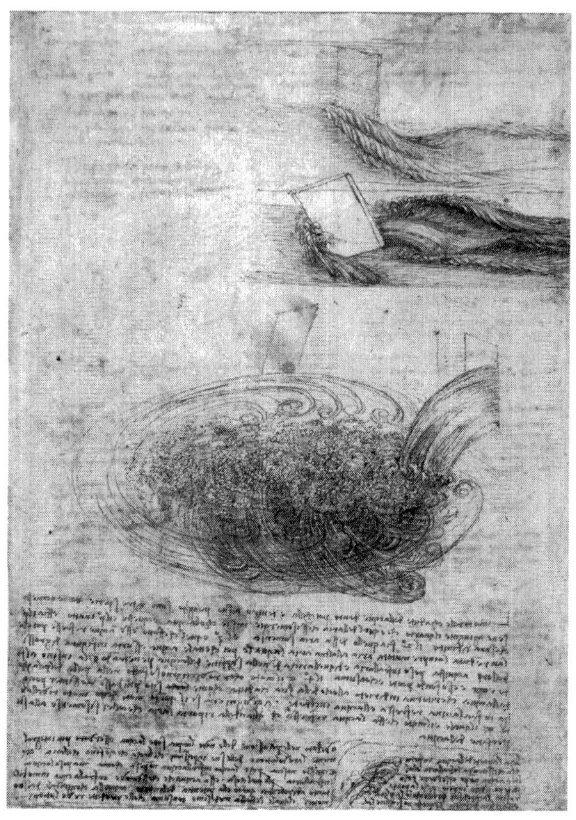

In *reading* a Leonardo painting, it is important to bear these two aspects in mind. One can start, as we did in *The Last Supper*, with the dispersal of the metaphysical organization in pictorial space and proceed to its exceptional orienting point (Christ). Alternatively, as in the following, one can begin with the latter and see how it relates to the hierarchical and centralizing organization that has been dispersed. A further consideration is that the paintings always waver between anxiety in zones of dispersal and separation (e.g., the space between mother and child in *St Anne*) and an enigmatic calm withdrawal characterizing the new orienting exceptional point, the messenger of infinity, that both belongs to and does not belong to the dispersed world whose originating core (its "womb") it occupies. As such, the most fruitful readings might be those that start with either anxiety or enigmatic withdrawal and see how the rest of the painting is elaborated around them, even when, as in the case of the Mona Lisa, both aspects are equally marked in a single figure.

Let us, then, get to Leonardo's St Anne.

IN LOVELY BLUE

> In lovely blue blooms the steeple with its metal
> roof. Around the roof swirls the swallows' cry,
> surrounded by most touching blue. The sun rises high
> above and tints the roof tin. But in the wind beyond, silently,
> a weathercock crows. When someone comes forth from
> the stairs of the belfry, it is a still life. And though the form
> is so utterly strange, it becomes the figure of a
> human being. (From Hölderlin, "In Lovely Blue")

As we lift our eyes, we first encounter a large head, somewhat isolated, at the center of the painting, surrounded by a heavenly blue expanse, slanted and withdrawn. As at the beginning of Hölderlin's poem, one might think that the setting is Christian, that the azure signifies hieratic and hierarchical logic and Anne is at the summit of a *vertical* line of divine transmission and generation. Very soon, however, one realizes that the vertical axis does not dominate the painting, since our gaze, in a sort of *split* (thus already introducing unpredictability and disruption into a metaphysical unity of direction), is called upon to follow at least two trajectories, both of them horizontal. On the one hand, if we look behind and beyond the head, we find ourselves not in a unified realm we can understand as a symbolic heaven but in a geographically articulated, mountainous landscape under an earthly sky constituting an indefinite *horizon*. As in Hölderlin, the hierarchical heavens break apart into a sky-covered landscape characterized by the movement of *around*-ness (German *um*[7]); the gaze can roam from any point to any other without definite order. The lovely blueness covers the chain of mountains, which seem dispersed and are painted in Leonardo's signature *sfumato*. It opens an infinite and indeterminate landscape. Every rock and every mountain seems to come out of the blue (in a way reminiscent of Chinese landscapes, even if the opening they effect is in the context of a different logic), indicating their emergence as a singular and unpredictable formation. Inimitably Leonardian, the rocks and mountains are at once dreamily ungrounded and groundingly real.

In its modern logic, the dimension of the dream is that which enters or emerges from the experience of the loss of everyday orientation and reality: the exposure to a dimension, expressed by the surrounding blue here (a sky emptied of its gods, to evoke Hölderlin again), of the unmooring of the world, its groundlessness. If dreams have always meant the intrusion of a mysterious or enigmatic message into the everyday world, they now are neither the transmission of the secret language of the gods ruling the cosmos (as in their classical, oracular version), nor the vision of a transcendent, providential design (as perhaps in their Christian, visionary understanding). Instead, they signify the intrusion of the background groundlessness, the infinite openness of this world. Such background is not meaningful in itself so much as it activates the energy of origination of infinite possible meanings and orientations. Each rock and mountain coming out of the blue is thus like a dream message, an enigma, in that we are made to feel—not unlike as we do in the aforementioned presence of the unpredictable lines and drips of a Pollock—their origin in the open infinity of the world. Their emergence is thus not guided by any determined and orienting configuration, by no order of things, and they are thus inscribed by the enigmatic and senseless (which is nevertheless the originating background of meaning) infinite opening of the world. What we have been calling the landscape is this opening of a world without a determined, ordered configuration, and it is because of that absence of determination that landscapes, dreamily unreal, confront us as lacking a familiar reality that we know how to orient ourselves in.

Yet the inhabitants of the landscape are also concrete and real to an unprecedented degree, as the mountains and rocks jutting forth in unpredictable singularity (what we mean by the singular is that which comes out of the blue, lacking any pregiven plan) attest. Confronting us in excess of anything one might have expected (for there is no preconception we could have had of them, emerging as they do not according to any given order), they impose themselves on us out of themselves rather than in relation to us. To speak with Jean-Luc Marion, they are intuitions in excess of concepts, or in excess of our capacity to preconceive that which appears. The real, in this sense (the sense of the new realism immanent to the question of the landscape), is not what takes place as an ordered and recognizable realm (however detailed and rich in distinctions and differentiations[8]). Rather, the real is that which imposes itself beyond what we are able to preconceive and foresee, or even desire, thus gaining an independence, indeed an alienation, from us, and from our preconceived gaze, appearing for itself and out of itself. To appear out of the blue, to appear as part of the landscape, is to appear as singularly real but simultaneously ungrounded and dreamlike.

On the other hand, to return to the second of our split movements in relation to St Anne, our gaze is called not only toward the landscape but also into the space opened by her downward-cast face and half-closed eyes, to follow a horizontal descent where we encounter the Virgin, Child, lamb, earth, and, finally, an abyss into which we are in danger of falling. This horizontal trajectory, which as we have said breaks the vertical hierarchical line of the Christian St Anne, presents us with a story of loving attachment and painful separation—between mother and child, child and lamb—characterizing those whose lives hover over an abyss, an abyss that is nothing but the expression of our way of inhabiting a landscape understood as a groundless and infinitely open realm.

These dual trajectories, that of the rocky landscape under the blue sky, and that of the descent into painful separation among those connected by bonds of love and desire are interrelated, constituting the two main aspects of the painting's break with Christian verticality.[9] In order to understand the interrelations, it is enough, at least to begin with, to inquire into the adventure our eyes have been undergoing, to follow the implications of their movements and their aims.

Our eyes first zoom in on St Anne's face as the largest and most central feature of the painting (thus occupying the heart of a field that, due to its decontextualized nature, strikes us with an originary helplessness and disorientation), as if seeking from her an answer to their anxiety; however, the design prevents the eyes from following the orienting vertical, hierarchical line, to which they may have been historically accustomed and whose task was to bring order to and diffuse the primordial anxiety—an anxiety it is the intent of the pictorial surface to reignite as if bringing us back to a primal scene. Instead, the eyes are called to move beyond and above St Anne, thereby losing themselves in the dizzying freedom from determination that is the surrounding, infinitely blue landscape. It is important to note how this *call to move beyond* and above Anne is inscribed in her enigmatic countenance. Not facing us directly or even looking with open eyes, she does not let us rest our gaze on her but rather draws us in by promising release from anxiety but refusing us access by withdrawing from us. Her smile seems to promise an answer that it at the same time refuses; we are forced to press onward, into the infinitely blue landscape, in search of answers she will not provide. In consequence, the landscape and her face infuse and inform each other: the infinity of the landscape becomes something that her enigma, her withdrawal without answer, expresses, and conversely, the infinite blue acquires her enigmatic character and becomes a site filled with desire.

At the same time, Anne's face itself almost seems to become one of the mountains. Like them, it seems to come out of the blue, in a dreamily unreal/real alienating strangeness, striking us with a troubling foreignness and its impression of being separate from us. As an expression of the landscape, St Anne becomes its messenger and transmitter. Through her paradoxical welcome-that-is-refusal (a smile combined with an averted gaze), we encounter an enigmatic expanse denying clear answers and meaning. Anne is thus a messenger of a dizzying freedom that arrives (the freedom, that is) complexly, since it arrives as a mixture of promise, desire, alienation, and frustration. She is an emissary of our freedom as infusing us—with the means of her enigmatic face, which simultaneously extends a promise as a privileged locus by which we may orient ourselves with regard to infinity and enacts a refusal—with the infinity of the landscape, but she is no less an emissary of painful separation: by refusing to provide a full answer (while eschewing an outright rejection) to the demands of our anxiety, she forges a bond of attachment even as she makes us detach ourselves from her. Separation is the experience taking place in a twofold movement, that is, between the attachment we effect to this exceptional locus of orientation within infinity and the withdrawal of this privileged site from being a full answer, which, *as withdrawal,* becomes the transmission of infinity and the origin of our desire (desire being simultaneously the infusion with the infinity of the landscape and the search for full answer from our locus of attachment).

That to which we are the most attached, that which—never giving us a satisfying answer—remains inevitably in excess of us, is also that in relation to which we feel the utmost separation. Attachment and separation are not opposed but occur simultaneously: the more we are attached to what exceeds us and, as such, infuses us with infinity, the more we feel separated from it. This painful separation, emerging in tandem with our opening to the dizzying freedom of the landscape in its infinite blueness, is nevertheless also a moment of partial safety, in that the exceptional locus is something to which we nevertheless remain attached, and passionately, if frustratingly so. However tenuous and painful, it is because of that attachment that we are not cast completely into the groundless and disorienting infinity of the landscape.

Wavering between separation and attachment, promise and frustration, origin of desire and/as refusal of satisfaction, Anne functions simultaneously as a promise of home, that is, a place of sheltered dwelling, and agent of exile. This exceptional, privileged figure within the construction of the painting thus plays a maternal role, and Anne herself is very much presented as a mother. She embodies the site where we come to inhabit the landscape: from her we receive a partial, privileged locus so we are not completely lost, falling into an infinite abyss without ground. At the same time, inasmuch as she refuses to provide a full answer, she grants a certain independence, "throwing us out" to be on our own. Serving as our origin in the landscape, the messenger of its infinity (thus being a finite-infinite agent), the exceptional Anne is fully intimate to us, that is, occupying the very core and center of our being, functioning as the source of who we are, yet at the same time this intimate origin remains external to us and can never be appropriated by us. Our intimate origin thus occupies our core as a fundamental, irreducible alienation. Anne is our heart and source, but a heart that always remains foreign and separate.

Another aspect of Anne's separate foreignness is that, as the site of our birth *into* the landscape, she can never be a regular part *of* the world or of the landscape. By virtue of being an origin, she thus remains in excess of every ordinary inhabitant of the landscape. As an intimate alien that is the origin of our world yet remains always external to the world and in excess of it, Anne acquires the character of what we have called an Image: an intimate ex-centricity that stands at the very origin and threshold of the world, or origination of the world in us. The Image is that part of the world that is also apart from it, in that it is the locus of its origin, or origination. It is both the most intimate to us yet also the place of our most disturbing alienating separation, since it is a separation at the place where we demand absolute attachment and response. The maternal locus, the place of our origin and birth in and into the landscape/infinite world, is an Image (namely, a messenger of infinity, a site of intersection of the infinite openness of the landscape and a finite occupant of the landscape), rather than a regular occupier of the world. The task of painting is to activate this originary Image in us, making us experience the recurrent and repetitive birth of, and into, the world, the place through which we are infused with the world, by becoming simultaneously attached to and detached from a privileged locus in it. The Image is thus simultaneously the place of our attachment to the world and the place through the painful detachment from which we are thrown on our own, inhabiting the world as cut off from any orderly continuity.

This paradoxical dual nature or aspect of the maternal Image, which is simultaneously intimate to us and external to us, I have characterized as an interlace, to borrow a term from Merleau-Ponty, and in earlier chapters as extimacy, a term taken from Lacan. Such a configuration of interlacing outside and inside marks the way that Anne and her daughter Mary are implicated in the painting. They are not exactly two separate figures, nor one single figure, but a strange hybrid of regular figure (as a particular inhabitant of the world) and Image (as the external intimate origin) that is neither two nor one.[10] Mary is intimately attached to Anne, her mother, being the exceptional origin through which Mary comes to be herself as occupier of the landscape, yet this attachment is also a detachment, never being a full fusion. In this sense Mary's interlacing with Anne, the exceptional origin, parallels or mirrors our own, spectatorial relation to the maternal Anne. Anne/the Image, we saw, anchors us even as her refusal infuses us with the infinite blue of an alien landscape.[11] Thus we ourselves become a hybrid figure/Image, or an interlace of image and figure, where the Image/painting is intimate yet external to us.

This transition to Mary, as a parallel figure to our own spectatorial experience, allows us further to understand the horizontal descent, the movement of painful separation and dispersal opening around Anne, which breaks the hierarchical trajectory of medieval representation. Our attachment to Anne—which also brings our detachment as infusion with infinite blueness—in a way opens in us an abyss. It removes the ground beneath our feet (the abyss at the bottom of the painting) and provokes a certain experience of falling from the sky.

The logic of such a scene is that it transmits itself: it opens a chain in which each attached/detached figure becomes in turn the source of attachment and detachment for the next. Mary, having been infused with infinity at the same time as suffering separation, remains connected with Anne, but due to her detachment and rejection by the enigmatic Image from complete fulfillment (i.e., from receiving a complete answer to the enigmatic desire with which she has been infused), she is in search of a new bond, which she finds in her child (a child that will be *a* Christ, or a Leonardo, as we will soon see, owing to the new relation to the Image that it will be his task to fulfill). Because Mary now embodies enigmatic, infinite desire, she wants both to attach the child to herself as well as to detach herself from him. Accordingly, the gesture she makes of reaching is suspended between trying to bring the child to her and letting him go. She is the source of his exile and loss of home, as well as the origin of his independence and exuberant freedom—the freedom of inhabiting an infinite groundless world, the anxiety and joy of which is very much felt in his movement.

The child itself is even more caught up in the tensions of the maternal transmission of infinity originating in/as the Image. He seems simultaneously released into his own, autonomous existence and called back home, for his gaze is cast backward even as he seeks a new object of attachment, the lamb.

The lamb of course represents a highly complex field of tensions. It is a sacrificial beast, whose extinction is supposed to bridge the gap between finitude and the infinity communicated by the mother, which remains in excess of any finite inhabitant in the world. Only a finite inhabitant of the world, used and consumed in a ritualistic way, can be the response to, and communication with, an otherwise ungraspable infinity. In this capacity, the lamb, *Agnus Dei*, portends Christ's passion: the sacrifice that will take away the sins of the world. Seen from the context of a hierarchical medieval cosmology (and thus in the context of the metaphysical idea of paternal centralization), sin itself is a specific interpretation of the infinite excess of desire communicated by the mother. Desire—from a position dominated by the metaphysical idea of paternal centralization—is a dangerous, sinful, disturbance. It is the task of sacrificial consummation to cancel out desire's sinful excess.

Yet in the context of a horizontal landscape, rather than that of a hierarchical medieval cosmology, the lamb (the figure, we should note, the furthest from the vertical line of Anne) points toward a logic that exceeds the metaphysical drama of scapegoating and sacrifice (i.e., the drama within the context of which the excessive infinity communicated by the mother is seen as a destructive and sinful danger). For the lamb in the landscape is a *real* lamb rather than the *symbolic* lamb of the Christian sacrificial drama (like that in Van Eyck's *Adoration of the Mystic Lamb*, for instance). It "speaks" for itself and emerges freely out of itself—and not in relation to the sacrificial desire of tradition. Thus we can say that the lamb suffers for itself, too. The lamb's fear of falling is not suffering of a symbolic, sacrificial nature but real suffering, the expression of an encounter with the groundlessness of the world and its treacherous abyssal nature.[12]

The fact that Leonardo's lamb is no longer symbolic does not mean that it should now be understood solely as one more occupant of the real world. Rather, Leonardo's lamb, in its interruptive realness, connects to the entire problem of the Image and represents a key element in the liberation from metaphysics. The lamb here is a key logical operator (i.e., one in whom the stake of the whole is inscribed). Its intervention in the painting—the way in which it shifts the drama of separation, resisting, so to speak, or separating itself from, being included in it, or at least fully included in it, as a sacrificial member—decisively interrupts the metaphysical verticality and exposes us to a new vision of the whole as infinite and unpredictable opening, to the world as landscape. This significance is underlined by the fact that the lamb represents Leonardo's addition to the traditional iconography of St Anne. As we have seen, it is an addition that pulls our gaze, in the most extreme manner, in a horizontal direction, away from the traditional verticality found in most treatments of St Anne. Paradoxically, we might say, the addition of the lamb, its surprising and unprecedented entrance, liberates us from sacrifice (an extension of sorts of the Abrahamic story where the appearance of the ram liberates from human sacrifice). The lamb is a de-sacrificial lamb.

What takes the place of sacrifice is play, specifically, the play of the world. Although the lamb could be said to function as a new object of possessive attachment as compensation for the detachment from the mother, from another point of view the child's encounter with the lamb expresses a newfound freedom: the transformation of detachment and separation into the encounter with the infinite potential of the world. The lamb comes from the world itself, in excess of any possessive desire of the child, and the joyful discovery of this surprise brings child and animal into a ludic relation: the suspension of determinate configurations and open-ended experimentation. This free openness is expressed in the horizontally winding path aligned with the child's head, extending toward the unknown woods. It is potentially a source of anxiety, but it is also the sign of unpredictable adventures, where the child and his new playmate, the lamb, can ride off together.

While the child's actions can be interpreted as the attempt to dominate and tame the lamb, subjecting the freedom of an occupant of the world to human desire—there is an irreducible violence in grabbing the animal's ears—to me this seems not the main component of the mounting gesture. For in mounting the lamb, the child is in the midst of experimenting with the terms under which he and the lamb can entertain their relations and experience their new togetherness in the world (the lamb itself is also a participant in this experimentation, as if also opening up, from its point of view, to the encounter of the unpredictability of the world). It is as if the mounting gesture is an expression of the way that, in entering an unpredictable relation, the two playmates are jointly setting out on an adventure on uncharted terrain, the adventure of the play of the world.

This ludic activation of the unpredictable infinity of the world—the fact that all its inhabitants come out of the blue and have to establish a togetherness that is never given in advance—starts with Anne, the mother/Image as messenger of infinity. Within the traditional, metaphysical system, the excessive infinity that we have argued characterizes her is experienced as painful separation; unfulfilled desire is to be transformed, by means of sacrifice, into an ordering vertical hierarchy. By contrast, in the new "system," that of the infinite play of the world, excessive infinity is something not to be dominated but a source of pleasure, the pleasure of experimenting with what exceeds us and is to remain as excess. Only once we liberate ourselves from the metaphysical sacrificial transformation of excessive infinity, and expose ourselves to the playful experimentation with the unpredictable opening of the world as landscape, do we fully open up to the Image, to Anne in her enigma as a giver of infinity. The opening up to the Image as a source of the play of the world transforms Anne/the Image from occupying a position in metaphysical verticality into a source of unbounded freedom. Such a transformation is the most essential task of modern painting. It is in this liberation into the full experimental freedom of the Image that is expressed in the child becoming *a* Christ, and the lamb, its counterpart, a de-sacrificial playmate.

Christ, which as we have mentioned was understood by the tradition as an Image (where the Image was still understood metaphysically and sacrificially), is here the playful redeemer *into* the Image in its enigmatic truth, which also means the redeemer of the world. He is thus the one who allows us finally to enter it *as* world, an infinite and unpredictable realm of experiment and experience. It is in this opening to the world as realm of play that the paradisiacal nature of the painting, its unmistakable (if highly ambivalent and complex, due to the various streams of possessive desire, traumatic loss, etc. present in it) idyllic and pastoral nature, consists. Gaining paradise is not the departure from this world to join another one but the attainment of unprecedented freedom in this world, achieved by transforming the world's infinity into an experimental, playful pleasure. Ultimately, gaining this adventurous pleasure is shown to be the aim behind the paradigmatic manner of forming our gaze by taking it on a circular path that is characteristic of all of Leonardo's major works: from Anne and the sky, along a horizontal descent toward the child Christ and the lamb, down the winding road of freedom toward the woods, then back to Anne, reconnecting to the infinity-giving, abyss-opening Image—only to descend again and reexperience the playful reopening of the world, in a circular eternal return.

It is in the irreducible nature of this world, in its infinite groundlessness, to hover over an abyss—hence the bottom of the painting—but it is in the full discovery of the Image that a new type of grounding can also be found: hence Anne's grounding feet, which allow the whole group to be secure, at least partially, from falling. This grounding is not an anchor in metaphysical substance but the capacity for play enabled by the Image's liberation into itself, a liberation allowing the abyss of the world to be the source of a constant, and unpredictable, creative reopening.

Chapter Four

The (Self-)Portrait of Modernity (*Mona Lisa*)

Who is the Mona Lisa?

By most accounts, the portrait we know as the *Mona Lisa* is the likeness of one Lisa Gherardini, the wife of a wealthy merchant who commissioned Leonardo to make the painting. Her enigmatic strangeness fascinated Leonardo so much that he continued to work on the portrait for more than a decade. However, numerous other speculations persist as to the secret of Mona Lisa's identity, among the most famous of which is that Leonardo depicted himself in disguise. Marcel Duchamp and Salvador Dalí, as pictorial interpreters of the painting, famously altered the image to present their own self-portraits (among other things). *Mona Lisa, c'est moi*, they seem to say, to vary Flaubert's remark on his own creation, Madame Bovary.

Is the *Mona Lisa* a mysterious stranger, the subject of the most famous of all Western pictorial portraits, or is she an enigmatic mirroring device through the interaction with which each and every person can come to open up to their own self and in effect say *c'est moi*? She is, I suggest, both, and it is the unrivaled precision with which Leonardo creates an exact point of interaction between the moment of portraiture (understood as the moment of the encounter with the enigma of a stranger) and the moment of self-portraiture (the moment of engagement with the enigma of one's self, or with one's own strangeness) that constitutes the *Mona Lisa*'s paradigmatic place in the history of painting.

It is the question then of the relations between the enigma of the stranger and the enigma of one's self that is at the heart of this most popularly celebrated (its popularity indicating its success in addressing everyone, its unparalleled universality) pictorial enigma.

Figure 4.1. Leonardo, *Mona Lisa. Source*: Wikimedia Commons, CC public domain.

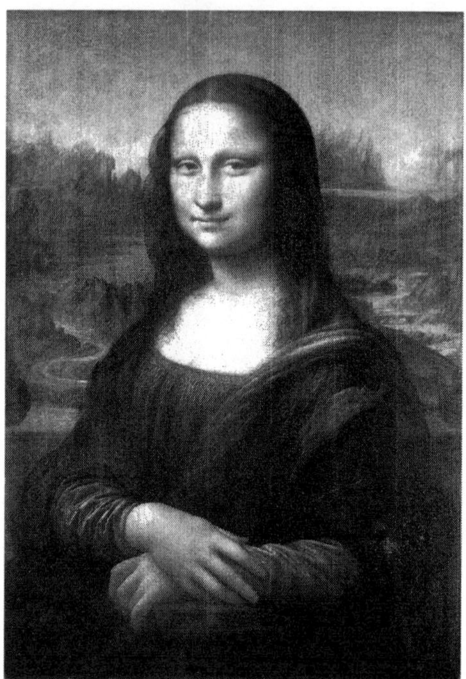

Let us start with the question of the enigma of the stranger. Who is the stranger? And how does Leonardo conceive of painting as the medium for the appearance of strangers in their enigma, that is, in the ungraspability of their identity, or in the withdrawal of their identity from precise determination?

Taking a look at the *Mona Lisa* as an enigmatic stranger, we can say that the stranger is the one who does not belong, who does not fit in as a recognizable element within the surrounding context and exceeds any frame of reference that would determine an appropriate place. Even before we look in detail we can see that Mona Lisa is strangely disproportionate relative to the frame; she is extremely close to the sides and the top, as if she could not be contained. One has the impression that she is, as in a cinematic close-up, too near for our gaze to take her in.[1] As in cinematic close-up, the subject is decontextualized, cut off from the context: Where is she? We don't know. What is her relation to the landscape behind her? We can't really say. What are those fragmented things that seem to occupy the edges of the wall in the background? A mystery. And what is the enclosed space she occupies? A balcony? A studio prop? Unclear. Where exactly is she looking? The painter, a studio guest, a passerby—or is she lost in a reverie? Needless to say, we can't tell.[2]

The close-up has the effect of subtracting and adding simultaneously. The more the context is removed, the more each trait of the subject seems to be erased and struck by spectral blankness. Yet this process can also be described as involving a positive dimension: something seems to have been added to what has been decontextualized, as if an invisible cover has been laid over it as a mysterious obstruction, which prevents us from situating it in a recognizable context, a cover that moreover seems to endow the decontextualized element or scene with a new, enigmatic, power. Leonardo places emphasis on this covering by giving Mona Lisa an almost transparent veil, as if to suggest that her mystery has to do with an addition of invisibility. The diaphanous piece of cloth is nothing substantial, but it represents an event in the dimension of meaning, namely, the dimension of the understanding of things in their relational context. The enigma, the occlusion of meaning, is the invisible cover added to the decontextualized subject of the close-up. By losing determination, the decontextualized gains in enigma.

Charisma is the traditional term for this phenomenon. The charismatic individual—exemplarily, a movie star—is a blankly enigmatic person who, withdrawn from graspable determination, seems to shine (an aspect we will return to below) with an enigmatic power.[3] Mona Lisa's face in close-up, and, by extension, the whole painting—a cutoff surface detached from the context of the world—is thus a surface covered by an enigma, charismatically shining with a new power. To gain in enigma, although it involves an emptying loss (which can be a loss of attachment, thus of a determining relation, as in mourning,[4] a loss of place of belonging, etc.), is then to gain in power. This is the case since power is that which marks an excess of potentiality over any actualized determination. As such, those who gain in enigma (Mona Lisa, movie stars) become the site of an opaque potentiality that is nothing but the potentiality to make new and unpredictable relations, the potentiality to communicate, in excess of every specific act of communication. Needless to say, such shining charismatic power is also unfailingly erotic, eros being an essential manifestation of that pure potentiality to be, or to communicate.

We can also call the power of communication the medium of communication, for it stands beyond any specific act of communication and makes such an act possible in the first place. We can understand this powerful shine as the appearance of a special kind of "light" (as in the famous light emanating from Moses as he descended Mount Sinai): not an object that appears but a medium that illuminates, thus which allows objects and specific meaningful configurations to appear. The shine is the becoming active and present of the medium of communication, an illuminating medium that is itself invisible, for it is not any actual content, yet nevertheless, somehow, at the moment of the event that is the work of art (as well as exceptional religious moments as the example of Moses alluded to), can itself be said to appear.

The shine is the charismatic, paradoxical appearance of invisibility, of the pure power to communicate. The enigmatically withdrawn subject of the close-up therefore constitutes a paradox: an actual thing that, in its withdrawal from determination, becomes the vehicle through which the medium discloses itself. This appearance, or appearing, of the medium is different in nature from any content that appears with the means of the medium, or through the medium. In fact, the appearance of the medium is not the appearance of a content but rather the activation of a power: the power to see meaningfully, to encounter things as part of a contextual and relational configuration.

The withdrawn, charismatic enigma that is the *Mona Lisa* starts to disappear as an element in the field of vision only to gain a new kind of radiance though which we are given power to see in a different light. This radiance, the event through which a power of seeing is communicated to us, springs from the withdrawn, enigmatic subject of the close-up, which functions as the messenger and communicator of the medium,[5] indeed, as the medium of the medium.[6]

It is vital to note that this radiance is something we receive, not something we possess. It is a power in relation to which we are initially passive and in which we come to participate. We receive the power to see by first being seen, that is, coming to occupy the place of those to whom the medium is transmitted from elsewhere. What we can call the moment of the Image, the event it is the task of painting to herald, is the moment of the charismatic communication of the shine by which we are seen (i.e., by which we come to occupy a field open to the power of vision) and through which we receive our power to see, or through which we might be said to be born into vision.[7] It is a blinding moment, in a sense, for we can receive our power to see only by being deprived of any determinate object of seeing or perception and by standing exposed to the nothing (or no-thing) that is the medium as such. Painting is the paradoxical event through which, by being deprived of the object of perception, by losing it in a way, we are given the gift of the power of vision. The moment of the image is a moment of loss and birth, mourning, and the gifting of the world, all of which the *Mona Lisa* stands for.

It is for good reason that the feature of the *Mona Lisa* to have been most widely remarked upon and celebrated is her smile, this essential moment in the activity of the mouth as medium of communication, which, without fail, is qualified as "enigmatic." This smile is a gesture of withdrawal from any actual utterance or communication, yet it harbors the power of speech as such. There are, to be sure, other gestures of the mouth, notably the cry or scream, where what we can view as speech-as-such is inscribed beyond any specific utterance, but these cases involve negative experience, a traumatic loss of the capacity to speak: being silenced against one's will. In the *Mona Lisa*'s enigmatic smile, by contrast, speech as such, or perhaps simply language, is evidently associated with a sort of satisfaction. Her expression is positive; the moment of withdrawal from determination and the passive reception of the shine are affirmed and embraced (rather than fought against as an unjust deprivation with which we have been afflicted) as our most proper negative power (in the sense of negation and emptying of any actual determination). We can speak of it as "most proper" even if it is disappropriating power (namely, as something we receive from an elsewhere), which undetermines us and is not in our control, since it is the power that, though we can never possess it, comes to define us most essentially. In the smile the negative power of speech or language is welcomed.

But further distinctions are required. Although the *Mona Lisa*'s smile evinces satisfaction and welcome, it cannot be described as satisfying and welcoming to us. Her smile is not the wide, welcoming smile that would satisfy us, as if fulfilling us, or reflecting to us the fulfillment of our desires, becoming an accommodating mirror. To the contrary, her withdrawn smile (which is perhaps not even a smile: the ambiguous indeterminacy of the mouth prevents us from being sure) is also withdrawing from us, from our capacity to grasp it and satisfy our wants through it. As such, in a way, it rejects us. Only in such evasive withdrawal can speech as such be in fact welcomed and satisfyingly express itself, that is, truly appear for itself and out of itself. For, if the "smile" would have satisfied us, it would have achieved a determination. It would have accommodated our specific wants and given us the illusion of reciprocity rather than express what is beyond any specific and determined want and thus beyond any mirroring reciprocity.[8]

The moment of the Image, then, the moment of the shine, is also always the moment of the birth, and the reception, of the power to speak, to communicate meaningfully. If painting is essentially an art of muteness—and this is one of Leonardo's key discoveries—it does not mean that it is withdrawn from language and speech; rather, it is an art that serves as a site for the birth of speech as such (and there is no need to associate speech exclusively with the utterance of words—one can speak visually, haptically, etc., i.e., activate any of the senses meaningfully). Almost all of Leonardo's paintings, most emphatically *The Last Supper*, with its staging of Christ's utterance, and the *Mona Lisa*, pose the question of the relationship between the muteness of painting and the birth of speech. It is not that the *Mona Lisa* needs, as the expression goes, *être belle et se taire but rather être belle et nous apprendre à parler vraiment*, namely, *nous donner la parole en tant que beauté enigmatique*, that is, in her enigmatic, silent, beauty, be the one through whom we receive speech, or are born into speech.

The withdrawal from any actual utterance and the accompanied inscription of speech as such can be designated by another essential term in this context: the secret, a term that also unfailingly accompanies descriptions of the *Mona Lisa*. The enigmatically withdrawn person who shines with charisma is invariably supposed to hold a secret, as the case of all celebrities proves (and there is no greater celebrity than Mona Lisa—as even Beyoncé recently demonstrated!). However, it is not a matter of secret meaning, which the person withdraws or withholds from us, a content that remains hidden,[9] so much as the source of meaning, the medium. The secret is the withdrawal from sense that obscurely shines as the excess over and above every concrete instance of signification: pure communication itself in its radiant moment of withdrawing from appearance.

Yet the mouth, of course, is part of that mysterious surface we call the face. What is the face, as Leonardo, by putting it in close-up, among several strategies, interprets it for us? It is an enigmatic surface, like painting itself, which can withdraw itself (or through which the self can express its own withdrawal) from any determination, becoming the place of habitation of pure communication, or the medium in excess of any determinate content and meaningful utterance. In the face the self shines forth, that is, it expresses its power of being a medium. Paradoxically, the face is that which can somehow possess the power of self-effacement: by enigmatically smiling, for example, and suspending any actualization and determination of meaning.

It is essential for any truly successful withdrawal from determination and meaning that we can never be certain whether something is actually withdrawn or not, and thus actually conveying a specific meaning or determined content. For were we not left in such a moment of suspension, we could determine something as withdrawn and no longer pay attention to it, and as a consequence we would lose the moment of the shine. Only through our uncertainty and hesitation can the shine become present and powerfully fascinate. It is vital, then, that we never know for certain whether the *Mona Lisa* is actually smiling (her smile, her secret, *is* this hesitation).

Leonardo has revolutionized the appearance of the face—that human surface in which the question of one's identity is most importantly inscribed within the realm of the visual and where the self comes to shine—by endowing it not with clear features and contours but with an indeterminate ambiguity. Chief among his means for doing so is his technique of sfumato, which introduces, in principle, limitless gradations, thus preventing us from determining where something begins and ends, where something is coming from and where it is heading. Leonardo thus turns the face into an arena of infinite shadings, of ambiguous plays with appearing (being on the verge of being determined) and disappearing (withdrawing from the almost achieved determination) that leave us forever in suspension. Only through such play with appearing and disappearing (and it is of the essence of play to leave us in suspense regarding determination) can the face cast its radiance, becoming the site of what exceeds the phenomenal world, the site of appearance of the medium as such. It has been noted that in the moment their death approaches, thus the moment of their worldly disappearance, the dying sometimes come to shine powerfully, a shine often described as a mysterious aura, an observation made as well about the moment of birth. Both these limit cases are thus always present in the moment of the Image: the pure shining of the self as medium at the moment of its communication and transmission, the moment of its radiation and illumination.

Leonardo's approach should be distinguished from making the face a blank receptacle for the divine, as is the case for medieval paintings (though the golden auras surrounding the countenance of saints can be said to express the radiance of the face at the moment of its worldly limit), where the face is withdrawn from determination as well, and, in fact, from any psychological traits. As we saw in the previous chapter, the blank face of traditional Christian art indicates how the pictorial surface serves as a moment of transition between two ontological levels, the visible (or phenomenal) and the invisible (understood as otherworldly substance). In the blankness of the face in medieval paintings, it is as if we are able to see or experience the effacing of the visible world and its psychological determinations and the transcending to the invisible beyond.

In contrast, the decontextualization of the *Mona Lisa's* face does not point to an invisible, substantial beyond but rather makes the invisible medium (which is not a substance but simply the openness of and to the visible) itself appear. The blankness of the *Mona Lisa's* face activates the medium in its pure state, becoming the site that is the origin and birthplace of appearance. Put another way, it is where appearance appears. Unlike the depsychologizing flat blankness of the face in medieval painting, the Leonardian face displays psychological depth, the mystery of modern subjectivity. Depth is the effect of being drawn in by something that withdraws from us, as into the eye of a storm (as we saw previously, a favorite figure of Leonardo), when that toward which we are drawn is experienced as the enigmatic, inexhaustible, and secretive resource of all that appears, and in fact belonging to that which appears, becoming an integral "part" of what it is. The invisible is no longer a separate substance from that which appears but is the medium of what appears, its immanent background.

The pictorial face as Leonardo develops it opens the realm where the invisible comes to belong to the visage and the visage comes to belong to its invisible background, which remains immanent to it. As such, the pictorial face discloses the secretive depth of appearance, thus where the medium comes to appear in its enigmatic radiance. This shining forth can also be described as the advent of modern subjectivity, understood as the event wherein the source and resource of one's appearance is no longer seen as a creative invisibility beyond the world but an infinite, secretive immanence.

The modern subject, it has often been said, is characterized by a new kind of interiority. We can understand such interiority as the effect of the blocking of accessibility, which characterizes the enigmatically withdrawn in whom the medium secretly shines. The medium, the no-thing, as excess over every configuration and every content, by definition does not allow access (it is a no-trespass zone, as the opening of *Citizen Kane*, that fundamental work dedicated to the relation between the Image, depth—in its famous use of the deep focus—and the inaccessibility of the enigmatic modern subject, famously constructs it). The medium is indeed beyond any determined relationship we might wish to entertain with it; the more we try to approach it, the more it escapes our grasp, leaving us with nothing. In this sense, the interiority of the enigmatic subject, its inaccessible depth, is exteriority.[10] This exteriority is the one that can be said to characterize the medium, indicating the fact that the medium can be described, to use a term of Gilles Deleuze, as the "absolute outside," that is, outside any positive content and meaning in the world.

The absolute outside is not the metaphysical outside of theological tradition, conceived as substance, but rather is nothing but the openness of everything in the world to everything else: the communicability of the world. Only with the coming to shine of this mediatic exteriority, on the demise of the substantial theologico-metaphysical exteriority, can the enigmatic interiority of the modern subject come to appearance. The *Mona Lisa* is one of the earliest and most radiant examples of such appearance.

This is not to say that this shining appearance of enigmatic subjectivity has simply arrived and now stands firm as our manner of life or being. Time and again, it has been shown, new metaphysical configurations are activated to prevent this from occurring. What Deleuze calls "reterritorialization" counteracts exposure to the mediatic nothing (an exposure resulting in the loss of metaphysical ground), by transforming the subject's relation to the world into a matter of calculation (among other techniques), thereby substituting a new ground for the old, theological one, and in that way defending against modern groundlessness. In a related process, the new, ungrounding nihil (i.e., the modern process of the annihilation of metaphysical ground) has opened room for the emergence of capitalistic subjectivity, which exchanges everything with everything else without cessation—a bottomless endeavor. The only new grounding power comes through amassing the groundless unit of infinite exchange, money, and founding an institution (a new church of sorts) that serves as the home for such amassing. In this doomed-to-fail defensive attempt, the bank provides the new ground for the subject of capital, transforming the nothing of the medium into something, that is, the groundless unit, which is an empty content that is nevertheless not nothing.

In the context of competing modern subjectivities, we can see the work of art, or Image, as the attempt to let a new kind of enigmatic subject shine in excess of the metaphysical subject grounded in the substantialized, metaphysical beyond and in excess of the assorted reterritorializing defenses with which modernity will ceaselessly try to dim the enigmatic subject's disturbing radiance. In distinction from the modern defensive efforts, it is with a smile that the work of art welcomes its own nihil and transforms it into a new, nonmetaphysical, grounding, creative power, the power of a play with nothing, upon which I have elaborated in previous chapters. It is true that the work of art has never managed to extricate itself fully from the realm governed by the various defensive modern subjectivities, nor has it itself been innocent of succumbing to their power, often confusing its own enigmatic shine with fetishistic shines created for the increase of the power of exchange.[11] Nevertheless, at its most profound the modern work of art as a medium of a new enigma, or as what I have been calling a new messenger of infinity, is the best guide on offer in the attempt to liberate ourselves from the various nihilistic subjectivities by which we have been overtaken, precisely because it offers, perhaps alone, a type of activity that involves a positive rather than a defensive embrace of the nihil.

But returning to the face: it is because the face is the main bodily site through which the self engages with the pure medium—engages with disappearance in order to be able to open (meaningfully) to appearance—that it is both the site of linguistic utterance and site of all the major senses (with the exception of touch, which characterizes the external body in its totality), but perhaps most importantly for painting, the faculty of vision.

What about the *Mona Lisa*'s eyes, then, this other celebrated element in her decontextualized face in close-up? They are often described in terms of paradox. On the one hand, it is unclear where they are looking, for they seem to be withdrawn from any determination. On the other hand, it seems that, no matter where the observer is, the *Mona Lisa* is always looking at them—indeed, seeing inside to the observer's deepest secrets. What is the relation between these two aspects? The key to understanding this is in the brilliant way in which Leonardo has designed the withdrawn nature of the *Mona Lisa*'s gaze. On the one hand, her eyeballs occupy the direct center of the horizontal line within which her face is placed. Because the pictorial space, as we have seen, is in essence decontextualized, and because, in addition, the *Mona Lisa*'s face is decontextualized, we are in a position of great disorientation, in search of a center to ground us, and the eyeballs thus come to serve as such center. The more we look for grounding in them, the more, looking directly at us, they seem to address us, to mean us.

But at the same time the centrally positioned eyeballs are located off center, and this in a double way. First, they are positioned at the left corner of the eyes, and second, the face itself, the context for the eyes, is slightly turned to the right while the shoulders themselves are not aligned with the face, since they are positioned at a sharper right angle. The effect is that the eyeballs, the face, and the shoulders, none of them in alignment with one another, are all off-center and in tension (in a more succinct version of the strategy Leonardo used in *The Last Supper*, in creating the tension between the dispersed apostles, as previously discussed). We have no way of determining which of them—eyeball, shoulder, or face itself—is the central and centralizing axis in relation to which the others are to orient themselves. In other words, none of them can claim centrality vis-à-vis the others.

This general decentralization, which renders the aim, and thus the centralizing orientation, of the situation undecidable, raises the question of movement. By presenting things off-kilter, as it were, the painting encourages the viewer to try to restore the balance, which can be done only if we start to imaginatively rotate, as it were, the eyeballs, eyes, face, and shoulders in various directions, so as to align them. Thus, we might be asking, is she about to turn her eyes and her eyeballs, together with the face to the right, to align them with the shoulders, or are the shoulders, face, and eyes in the course of moving leftward in the direction of which the eyeballs and their gaze have preceded them? Perhaps all the portrait's elements are headed in another direction still, each in a different rhythm? The uncanny dynamism that the figure of the *Mona Lisa* seems to have assumed[12] makes it impossible to determine the aim and meaning of her gaze. Is she looking at us from the center, as we might have been led to believe at first, or does she have an altogether different focus, in relation to which we are off-center? Of course, we can't say.

It is crucial to understand the import of such indeterminacy, which is all pervasive. If the *Mona Lisa*'s gaze were aimed in some indeterminate direction but did not seem to be looking directly at us, we could at least know that we are not the aim and meaning of her gaze. This would let us off the hook, so to speak: we would not be implicated in her disturbing withdrawal from meaning. Only if we cannot determine whether we are the aim, or address, of her gaze can we be said to be completely implicated in her estranging gaze (that is, a gaze introducing a strange foreignness into our relation to ourselves), become subjected to her enigmatic withdrawal. Only then is our identity, the question of who we are, which is the question of who we are in a contextual configuration,[13] at stake. If we were certain of being addressed (or certain of not being addressed) we could stay as we are. But if we are caught in this hesitation, the enigma infiltrates the very core of our being, exposing us in a new way to the problem of who we are. This hesitation as to whether we are addressed or not is the precise parallel to Hamlet's opening—and is, I suggest, an essential moment, perhaps even the essential moment, in the logic that opens modernity—with its famous "who's there?" For such a question responds to a prior disturbance, and it is unclear if the one who asks "who's there?" is the intended addressee of the disturbance or not.[14]

Having been infiltrated to the core of our being by the enigma (an enigma that is also articulated as the question to be or not to be, which is the question accompanying the hesitation: is it I who am intended or not?), the question of who we are having been raised with the utmost stakes, we are but one step away from realizing that we are, fundamentally, those who are called by the enigma, called by the pure medium as withdrawal from any determination. We are thus not who we are, for we are infiltrated by the power of an absolute negation: the pure medium as withdrawal from any determination. *Je est un autre*, as Rimbaud famously stated—the *autre* needing to be understood as the medium, that which is *autre* to any content and determination of the *je*.

In not being certain whether we are addressed or not, whether we are the aim of her regard or not, we are still addressed, we can say. That is, our identity is aimed at and at stake, but in a new way: we are now addressed by the enigma, becoming, as a consequence, an enigma (*autre*) to ourselves as well as an enigma in and to the world. The *Mona Lisa*'s uncertain gaze, which because of its uncertainty penetrates into the very core of the question of our identity, thus becomes that which "sees" into us most deeply, into the very secret of our being. She sees more of us, and otherwise, than we saw of ourselves, more than we knew about ourselves. The more she disregards us, the more we cannot grasp and determine her gaze, the more she penetrates us, with no escape. Through the ambiguity of her gaze, the Mona Lisa calls us back to our most fundamental "nature," to our enigmatic "essence."

Since it is the communication of her enigma that renders us enigmatic, the *Mona Lisa* (the modern Sphinx par excellence) can be described as the messenger of the enigma, through which we can be said simultaneously to be lost and found. Lost in terms of a specific identity that we have possessed or claimed prior to the encounter with her, found in that through her gaze, with the means of her gaze, we connect to the core of our being as an enigmatic "who?," as those inhabited by pure communication or by the pure medium of communication. This dialectic of lost and found can also be understood in terms of homecoming and exile. In estranging us, addressing us as those who are beyond anything we had been and known about ourselves, she exiles us, unmooring us from the place we have hitherto occupied, but in such self-exile she also brings us home, namely, brings us to our most fundamental sense of self. She is the enigmatic messenger of our being, calling us back to who we most fundamentally are, but this home is a site of absolute estrangement (in the sense that the medium that we become, and that we are, through her, is absolutely strange, absolutely *autre*, to any actual determination, being nothing but openness to various determinations).

Essential ambiguity characterizes what we can call the feminine address, in both an erotic and a maternal sense, a siren's song from a place beyond any determinate, paternal authority (and we can notice that the presence of the sea—an effacement of landed bearings—is essential in the painting, sending us to *The Odyssey*, with its questions of crisis of paternity, exile, and homecoming). As the promise of homecoming, the *Mona Lisa* provides an intense object of desire and love, but as the source of our loss and exile[15] she can become the object of our wrath, even something we may want to take revenge on, as Duchamp showed by defacing her by adding a mustache, as if wanting to turn her into an object of ridicule while at the same time making her into an object of iconic reverence, even if in the modality of violent desacralization. We want her all to ourselves—as demonstrated by the famous theft of the painting from the Louvre[16]—yet we also desire her destruction, as acts of vandalism directed at her through the years all too clearly demonstrate.

Atmospheres

But that is not all. The *Mona Lisa* as a messenger of the enigma, a kind of sea siren[17] (yet another relation to the question of speech and voice), is not alone in the painting, for she is, as the question of the sea already indicates, placed in relation to a no less enigmatic landscape behind her. We can characterize the landscape as atmospheric (Leonardo is perhaps the first to have evoked such landscapes within Western painting). What is the nature of the relations between the enigmatic Mona Lisa and the atmospheric landscape? The atmospheric and the enigmatic (and various additional terms that can be attached to them, such as the shadowy, the foggy, the moody, etc.) are essentially interrelated concepts, having to do with the effacement and covering of clear, determined meaning and orientation. The atmosphere, a word that originally referred to the vapors and gases surrounding a planet, names the effect of blurring and covering over any determination, thus any clearly grasped contextual configuration. A scene becomes atmospheric once a feeling of indeterminacy pervades it, where everything specific in it seems to become covered over by a displacing namelessness, an unplaceable excess (over any determinate content). In this sense, the atmospheric is immediately enigmatic, and in fact we can say that it is the becoming-present, to sensibility, of what we have called the medium, namely, that which is withdrawn from any specific determination, since it opens the whole. Leonardo's sfumato, which blurs the contours and precise limits of things, is an exemplary technique for conjuring and actualizing this atmospheric effect. If the artist's most important use of sfumato is in the creation of his dreamy and moody landscapes—the creation of scenes whose haziness we usually associate with the Romantic era, with the foggy marshes of Emily Brontë or with the paintings of Caspar David Friedrich—it is because his understanding of the landscape is atmospheric, that is, mediumistic.

The landscape is not simply a collection of things in nature but is the medium of the opening of and to things, a medium that becomes sensibly present above all as an atmosphere. Leonardo's painting, to an unprecedented degree in the West,[18] is dedicated to the landscape, that is, to depicting the mysterious appearance (mysterious to the extent that it is different from any regular appearance of actual things) of that which is the excess over and above everyday phenomena, what we have called the appearance of the medium of appearance, the atmospheric landscape. Painting is thus, we can say, the medium (i.e., that which enables the appearance of) of the medium, or the medium of the atmosphere. Like the *Mona Lisa*'s enigmatic face, the atmospheric landscape gives the feeling of an inaccessible depth. The depth of the landscape is not simply its receding into the distance but something beyond any distance, something that the growing visible distance, by making things ever more blurry and as if covered from vision, allows us to access, to make present. The feeling of depth in the landscape is the becoming present of the medium that is the landscape itself, in excess of its occupants. In the tradition of landscape painting a particular significance is attached to paintings devoid of human actors. As we have remarked, Leonardo's first known drawing, *Arno Valley Landscape*, is often considered the first pure landscape, with no human characters, in European art. Nevertheless, Leonardo seems to have always been interested in the relations between landscape and humans, especially the latter as what I have called the exceptional figure—exceptional since it has to do with the ex, with the outside or absolute outside as the medium—and the landscape. This is because he was fascinated by a new understanding of the human as a privileged, exceptional locus where the depth of the landscape secretly resonates: modern subjectivity (or one possible interpretation of modern subjectivity) as an unprecedented manifestation of an interiority (as inscription of absolute exteriority). The exceptional figure makes manifest, activates, and communicates the dimension of subjective interiority by being charismatic and withdrawn—escaping any determination, and thus any localization within the open world—and making the landscape as such shine forth.

We can see again that the outside (the absolute outside which is the atmospheric landscape as such, beyond anything that takes place in the landscape) is the inside, that which is most intimate to us, more secretive than any secret, our becoming exposed and open to the world, having been inscribed by the medium. The depth of the landscape is who the *Mona Lisa* is—and by extension, through her, who we are, most intimately and essentially. She is, and we are through her, an intimate exposure, "hiding" in our inexhaustible depths the outside that is the landscape as medium. To be or to have an interiority is thus to have the dimension of the landscape inscribed in oneself, yet inscribed as something inaccessible in oneself, beyond and before anything one can grasp, for it is the medium that enables any grasping and any opening to the world, thus to anything as part of a dimension of meaning and context. In this sense, the depth of the landscape is simultaneously farther away than any distance and closer than anything else in the world.

If the *Mona Lisa*, as a paradigmatic modern subject, one possessed by an unprecedented immanent depth, is someone in the interiority and intimacy of whom the depth of the landscape/medium resonates in a privileged way, it is because she can also be said to be the messenger of the landscape and its witness (not unlike, but to a more profound degree, the angel we analyzed in *The Annunciation*).

To emphasize and elaborate a bit, the Subject, the one in whom the depth of the landscape resonates, is both part of the landscape and stands apart from it—hence the *Mona Lisa*'s partial separation emphasized by the wall behind her, most literally, but indicated by every aspect of her withdrawal and decontextualization, which forbids us from locating and determining her in any way. To be the echo chamber of the depth of the landscape, that is, the place of resonance of the medium of the world, is the mystery of being both an occupant of the world, part of it—which Mona Lisa, as any finite being, is—but also not any determined part of it, since she is the taking place of the medium itself as well, which is by definition beyond any part, infinite. This is the sense of Walter Pater's famous words: "She is older than the rocks among which she sits; like the vampire,[19] she has been dead many times, and learned the secrets of the grave; and has been a diver in deep seas, and keeps their fallen day about her; and trafficked for strange webs with Eastern merchants; and, as Leda, was the mother of Helen of Troy, and, as Saint Anne, the mother of Mary; and all this has been to her but as the sound of lyres and flutes, and lives only in the delicacy with which it has moulded the changing lineaments, and tinged the eyelids and the hands." Neither dead nor alive, everyone and no one, but that medium that haunts the birth of all that appears in the landscape and its annihilation. The nothing from which everything emerges, she is a universal Mother (the real reason behind Freud's speculation that the *Mona Lisa* depicts the artist's own mother).

Mirrors

By being outside the landscape, withdrawn from any determined place, while at the same time occupying it, the *Mona Lisa* can be said to be the place of the inscription of subjectivity. This also means that she comes to serve as the site of an enigmatic address or call through which (namely, through her becoming a messenger of the landscape) we ourselves can be called to ourselves as enigmatic subjects, echo-chambers of the landscape-as-medium. Hereby, the *Mona Lisa* is not an object of our vision but its medium—like Christ in *The Last Supper*. Through her we can open both to ourselves and to the landscape, meaning open to ourselves as those who are the depth of the landscape, or as those in whom the depth of the landscape is inscribed as an inexhaustible and secretive interiority.

The process is exemplified by the way our eyes are made to move. Because we are denied access to the *Mona Lisa*'s secret, we are forced to look beyond her, as it were. In looking beyond we do not just see the features of the landscape (its "positive content"), but in or as the act of looking beyond, in becoming drawn by the depths, we become ourselves the depth of the landscape, namely, the medium of openness without any determined point of arrest. In addition, in passing beyond Mona Lisa toward the landscape, we encounter a terrain that allegorizes our own affective ambiguity, moving between warmth and cold, distance and intimacy. Inasmuch as she refuses our approach, the *Mona Lisa* becomes a cruel and distant ice queen (which the faraway white mountains, with their icy or snowy appearance, seem to express), cold to our desire and to our wish for a home in her—that is, a place of belonging and escape from disorientation—becoming the heartless agent of our exile. But at the same time, by opening us to the depth of the landscape as a messenger of infinity—of the medium beyond any specific finite content—she also bids welcome and offers a true homecoming;

we are permitted to come to our most fundamental self, beyond any false localization and alienating misperceptions, infused with the warmth of the hearth, a place of belonging.

In this way, the *Mona Lisa* grants, as it were, entry to the land with its warm browns as a place of human (i.e., mediumistic) habitation. The strokes on the ground (such as the winding road to the left of the painting), much like the strokes of the paintbrush, seem to indicate how the human being, the mediumistic creature, is to engage with the world or landscape of which it is a member, a (finite) part, but from which it is also apart. In drawing a stroke—which is, as every stroke is, a road leading toward the open sea, that is, toward that which indicates the indeterminate openness of the landscape/world—or in building a bridge (as found on the righthand side), the mediumistic creature both opens to the landscape in which it finds itself—emphasizing and articulating, as in the case of the road, the singular configuration by which the landscape is already characterized (the mountainous potential for the road was already there)—as well as exposes, as in the case of the bridge, the landscape itself to hitherto uncharted relations, connecting things that were not connected etc. The cold distance of the *Mona Lisa*, exiling us from any determined place that we might have occupied until now, also allows us to connect to our mediumistic essence, bringing us home and permitting us to inhabit the landscape as something of which we are a part and of which we are apart. The coldness ultimately radiates warmth—or the cold is that which allows us, as it does any spy, thus any exiled figure losing its place of habitation and becoming a watcher of the foreign, to come in to ourselves.

This logic of dispossession at the heart of coming-to-possess-ourselves guides the duality of the *Mona Lisa*, a duality with which we opened this chapter. She is both a foreign figure, an enigmatic stranger, and an invitation to self-reflection, an enigmatic mirror. Ultimately, she is the self-portrait of each and every one who engages with her. Her unique, exceptional foreignness sounds the call through which we come to ourselves as those who are in excess of every determination and position, those who are characterized as being a "who" question, namely, those who are exposed to the world as such before any determination.

The mirror, according to Lacan, poses the question of locating ourselves in what he calls the field of the Other. As we have seen, this needs to be understood as what is Other to any content: the medium as such, or the unpredictable openness of the world. To locate ourselves in the field of the Other is to negotiate between the finitude and determined actuality characterizing us as specific occupiers of the landscape, and the mediumistic infinity by which we are called, characterizing us as undetermined enigmatic depth. The (finite) one who needs to locate him- or herself in the field of the Other/the call of the medium is, by definition, Other to oneself (je est un autre, as we saw), haunted by an irreducible alienation, for she or he is (also) an absolute Other to any specific place or determination, any specific content (of the landscape). The problem of the mirror is that of the need to come to itself of the irreducibly alienated creature.

But whereas Lacan discusses the problem of the mirror in terms of achieving determination and self-recognizability, supposedly overcoming one's constitutive alienation (a false overcoming through which our essential Otherness is obscured, resulting in fundamental self-misrecognition), the problem of enigmatic mirroring (in the sense of that technique through which we engage with the problem of locating ourselves in the field of the Other[20]) as posed by painting, or the construction of a pictorial surface, concerns the very opposite: recognizing oneself as fundamentally alienated, not as someone in particular so much as an undetermined exposure to . . . a "who." The *Mona Lisa*, as enigmatic mirror, is that foreignness that in calling us to ourselves allows us to be, and to relate to ourselves as, those who are absolutely beyond, and Other, to ourselves, those whose intimacy is the depth of the landscape toward which we are drawn.

Conclusion

The preceding discussion of Leonardo's works has sought to follow a logical transformation of the Image, or the way in which the Image, understood as a phenomeno-logical surface—a surface made for the manifestation of logos, the manifestation of a Whole in which all phenomena find their place—changed function in passing from medieval Christian sacred image to modern painting. Whereas in the former the Whole to be shown was interpreted as static, composed of a substantial division between two vertically aligned realms—a sphere of invisible substance above, eternal and unchanging, ordering and governing the mortal world below—the vision announced by Leonardo, and the modern era at the threshold of which he stands, acknowledges no such division. Rather, the pictorial surface has the task of showing a new, dynamic Whole that opens horizontally, and what previously counted as a governing substance above this world is understood as the infinite, and unpredictable opening of this world, its blue background, so to speak, in the terms of our discussion of *St Anne*.

We have seen that in the context of the two phenomeno-logical systems the pictorial surface or space orbits around exceptional figures (the angel, Christ, St Anne, and Mona Lisa herself), which we can also regard as pictorial logical operators: intra-pictorial figures that stand as the messengers of logos, which I have also called messengers of infinity. The messenger is the point of communication between visible phenomena and the invisible logos, radiating a power around which all other occupants of pictorial space are organized. Understanding these messengers of infinity as those around whom the pictorial work (as a phenomeno-logical surface) revolves implies a distinct mode of looking that we can call as well phenomeno-logical. The paintings invite a gaze in line with the logos and with the manner in which the logos is inscribed in the pictorial surface. Looking phenomeno-logically means zeroing in where the messenger of infinity is located in the pictorial surface (we can extend this to all arts; within the context of each there are figures that can be understood as serving as messengers of infinity) and then following the way the rest of the pictorial surface or space is organized in relation to it. If in Christian sacred images the gaze zoomed in on the central sacred figures, for example, Christ or St Anne, in order to see how they function as the center of a vertical ordering, in Leonardo's paintings it becomes a question of grasping the way in which the pictorial surface is organized around the tension between a central figure/logical operator/ messenger of infinity and a field of anxious dispersal. The latter displays two aspects: first, the anxiety attending the loss of traditional vertical ordering, and second, the emergence of a new whole, which I have called the world-as-landscape, a groundless realm over an abyss. The anxiety expresses, from this perspective, the abyssal background of the world.

In the context of this abyssal realm, the exceptional figure provides a new center around which all other pictorial elements revolve; it can be understood as their source and origin, serving both as the transmitter and messenger of a new infinite opening, a new logos, and functioning as a new, nonmetaphysical ground, namely, as something that enables inhabitation of this newly opened realm by being a constant source (or resource) to which one can return in order to participate in the originating power of this open realm.

The phenomeno-logical "training" of our gaze demanded by Leonardo means becoming part of a circular movement that goes back and forth between the central logical operator and the dispersed figures occupying the pictorial surface. In this framework, the eye constantly connects to what grants the power of vision, that is, opens the gaze to a dispersed world of discovery. From origin to dispersal, and back again, the phenomeno-logically trained eye participates in the creation of the world and experiences the opening of its own power to see as an ever-renewed event.

Notes

Introduction

1. By "real images," I mean images in which reality is at stake, which happens only when the world as such, in its non-appearance, thus its withdrawal from visibility, comes to be what is in question.

2. Perhaps the most influential art historical study to have theorized the shift from medieval sacred images to Renaissance paintings (not specifically Leonardo's) distinguishing between what he understands as the era of holy images and the era of art is Hans Belting's *Likeness and Presence: A History of the Image before the Era of Art*, a book that has been much debated, challenged, etc., debates and challenges that are beyond the purview of the current book.

3. Of course, this is not necessarily true in actuality of all medieval and Renaissance works; however, it does characterize the most sophisticated and exemplary ones, and as such indicates that a logical conception of pictorial space became a possibility guiding the most ambitious and profound image makers.

4. I am collapsing various possible theoretical positions regarding this problem. For an important discussion of the matter regarding the question of the pictorial image in relation to the dual nature of Christ, see Charles Barber *Contesting the Logic of Painting: Art and Understanding in Eleventh-Century Byzantium*.

5. Erwin Panofsky has shown, in his famous *Perspective as Symbolic Form*, that Greek and roman paintings, for example, were also subjected to a certain demand for unity, though this demand was that of natural perception. In the medieval pictorial logic, a new type of a demand for unity has been introduced, he says, which I'm calling here that of the logos beyond nature and beyond the mechanisms of perception, a demand that we can thus name, literally, meta-physical, which in a way changes the entire character of the pictorial field.

6. "Unmasking the World: Bruegel's Ethnography," 245.

7. Of course, this a somewhat reductive view. As in medieval imagery, tension traverses the pictorial surface through and through—tension between, on the one hand, what we might call the demand of the image and, on the other hand, a metaphysical principle (divine reason in sacred images, geometry in Renaissance

painting), which demands a unity of a very specific kind (theological, geometrical) under the power of which the entirety of the pictorial surface is called upon to stand.

8. These formulations are indebted to the work of Jean-Luc Nancy, who develops the Heideggerian problematic of the world in an essential way.

9. Understood here as the pictorial task of showing and activating the logos, to be distinguished from the phenomenological as the modern term for philosophy beyond its metaphysical age, thus philosophy in the age of the thinking of (the unity of) the world (of appearance).

10. "Painter of the world" is to be distinguished from what Heidegger called the "world picture," which characterizes the modern age by his account. While the world picture concerns turning the unpredictable openness which is the world—an anxious openness increasingly haunting modernity upon the demise of the meta-physical theological grounding of the world of the Christian age—into a realm dominated by a calculative subject, a subject of representation seeking to dominate in advance (in a transformation of the logic of the providential creator) all that could possibly appear the modern project of the painter of the world is the very opposite: to release, by means of painting and the arts in general, the world into its own groundless, communicative openness. From the outset, then, modernity is caught between rival approaches to the fraught appearance of the world in the wake of the demise of the age of theology, the one scientific geometrical, as well as capitalistic (though the logic of capitalism and of science is different), the other we can call poetic: the one striving for a world picture, the other to bring about the world with the means of painting.

11. And the medium, by definition, is always beyond any content that appears through it, or with its means.

12. The painter who came closest to this insight, in the age just after Leonardo, is Giorgione, who was possibly influenced by his forebear's work, as Vasari claims. As Christopher Wood writes in *Albrecht Altdorfer and the Origins of Landscape*: "In Michiel's notes on Venetian painting, paese can still refer to an element of the picture, for example in the description of the 'foreground landscape' in Giovanni Bellini's St Francis Receiving the Stigmata, now in the Frick Collection. In other entries, however, the term paese becomes the primary identity of the picture: Giorgione's tela del paese cun el nascimento de Paris (landscape canvas with the Birth of Paris) or, again, the molte tavolette de paesi painted by Albert of Holland. Most remarkable is Michiel's description of Giorgione's Tempest as a 'paesetto on canvas with a tempest, a gypsy woman and a soldier' (proving that if there ever was a story, it had been forgotten only twenty years after Giorgione's death!). *From this point on it becomes possible to describe a whole picture as 'a landscape'*" (1993, 62–63, my emphasis).

13. Most of Leonardo's paintings are still in vertical format, yet the movement they introduce is in many ways horizontal, although tension between the two tendencies persists, and in fact, we might say that he is also a thinker of a new verticality, culminating in the mystery of his last painting, St. John. This verticality, I think, is of a new kind, which no longer points to a substantial beyond but to

a more enigmatic beyond-the-painting that depends on the new non-metaphysical horizontality. As Christopher Wood observes, "portable panel paintings were almost always vertical in format before 1520" (1993, 54).

14. I'm not saying that what Leonardo does is fully grasped with these concepts (themselves not entirely to be equated) of deconstruction of Christianity or profanation, but certainly they point to an essential direction in trying to understand his pictorial project that opens a realm that is neither theological nor secular.

15. Agamben, *Profanations*, 77.

16. It is important to note that what I'm calling Leonardo's logic of profanation developed in the context of many Renaissance attempts to escape the domination of various categories associated with hierarchical metaphysics, both in its Christian and Aristotelian articulations, with their emphasis on completed form, the primacy of narrative, causal action ordering one thing after another, work over leisure and play, etc. It was mainly in marginal works, not the important official and public ones, Christopher Wood has noted, that such attempts at escape were undertaken, often around the emergence of the question of the landscape. Only with Leonardo, I suggest, whose main works, rather than marginal ones, revolved around the question of the landscape, was a profound conceptual escape from metaphysics achieved, by means of a new systematically developed pictorial phenomeno-logy.

Chapter One

1. For an important discussion of Sfumato, see Alexander Nagel "Leonardo and Sfumato" (*RES: Anthropology and Aesthetics* 24: 7–20)

2. A framed space that we can associate with the logic of early Renaissance geometrical perspective. Daniel Arasse notes the desire to liberate from Renaissance geometrical perspectivism that already drives Leonardo in this very early painting, a perspectivism that the virgin as if still belongs to but which the landscape exceeds. See his *L'Annonciation Italienne*, 259–60.

3. In fact, from one perspective, the naturalistic wings could be understood in relation to technology, already heralding Leonardo's later experimentation with various flight mechanisms.

4. Or perhaps four if we take our own position to stand in for an additional, disappearing figure.

5. See my discussion of Leonardo's new understanding of the center in the chapter dedicated to *The Last Supper* and to the centrality of Christ in it.

6. Even the *Mona Lisa*, obviously a painting without an infant, can be said to participate in this relation in that it is in relation to her withdrawn face, as we will see, which communicates the world as landscape to us, that we are called to occupy, among other possibilities, the miraculous position of the arriving infants.

7. Or more precisely, to profanate, in the term we used in the introduction to describe the general aim of Leonardo's pictorial project. In fact, probably sensing

this were the case, those who commissioned the painting from Leonardo for a chapel in the San Francesco Grande church in Milan rejected the painting.

8. Or, in the terms of the introduction, as a threshold (to appearance) figure.

Chapter Two

1. For a particularity influential and erudite study of the transition from medieval images to modern painting, see Hans Belting's *Likeness and Presence: A History of the Image before the Era of Art.*

2. Indeed, "art," a term still attached to the metaphysical tradition, might not be a particularly apt word for the new place that images aim to have in human life and existence in general. Joseph Beuys has tried to go beyond the latter by talking about an extended concept of art. This seems to me the right direction, even if it does not yet go far enough.

3. And Leonardo was already an enigma for his contemporaries, as Vasari makes clear.

4. I am not using this distinction between mystery and enigma in any precise historical sense. The latter term has an ancient history and was used, notably by St Augustine, in relation to the problems of Christianity. However, it seems to have been of more use in the traditions of rhetoric and poetics from Aristotle onward (see Eleanor Cook, "The Figure of Enigma: Rhetoric, History, Poetry"), rather than Christianity, and as such points to something slightly different from Christian mystery: opacity that becomes present at the heart of the meaningful world *as* opacity.

5. Or perhaps more precisely as an umbilical cord allowing access to the mediality (the immanent beyond of every content) that is the world.

6. It has often been remarked that a tension exists in the painting between its geometrical grid and the dynamism of the apostles who do not fit into this grid.

7. Leonardo explored the event of a general loss of place, extraordinary commotion, and dramatic struggle in Battle of Anghiari, which was never completed and eventually destroyed.

8. As Kenneth Clark observes, "Unity and drama, these are, the essential qualities by which Leonardo's 'Last Supper' is distinguished from earlier representations of the subject." Moreover: "Evidently one cannot look for long at the 'Last Supper' without ceasing to study it as a composition, and beginning to speak of it as a drama. It is the most literary of all great pictures, one of the few of which the effect may be largely conveyed—can even be enhanced—by description."

9. It is often noted that one of Leonardo's main innovations in *The Last Supper* is to have introduced Judas into the group of the apostles without distinguishing him from them—in contrast to earlier depictions, where Judas occupied the other side of the table and thus was easily identifiable.

10. Leo Steinberg points to this strange quality of Christ as being, on the one hand, a hieratic figure and, on the other hand, what he calls a narrative figure.

11. It has been remarked that *The Last Supper* seems to uncannily belong and not belong to the room within which it was originally displayed. Due to Leonardo's strange use of perspective, in order to see the painting from a "proper" angle one would need to be positioned in the air rather than standing on the ground. We can thus see that the question of enigmatic belonging and not belonging is at the heart of the problem of the painting as Leonardo conceived it.

12. It is a recurrent question whether Leonardo already fully belongs to the modern age or is still part of the medieval period. While I do not have a general thesis to advance on the subject, I am following the intuition that as far as his thinking about images is concerned he transforms medieval logic, even if he points to something we might not fully associate with the logic of modernity (or what is taken to be its dominant feature: secularity). The enigma of Leonardo's paintings, I believe, concerns something we might think of as a third way in relation to the question of the Image, neither Christian, nor exactly modern or secular (and its associated terms, representation, subjectivity, expressivity, etc.).

13. We will later see that in a way nothing specific actually has to be lost in order for the Image to have the character of return from lostness. There is as if an originary loss the appearance out of which, or the return from which (a primordial resurrection), it is the task of the Image to bring about.

14. For example, the Christ-Image can be understood, in the manner of Freud's suggestions in his Leonardo essay, as the return of a childhood memory of Leonardo, abandoned by the father, then taken away from the mother, taking the shape of a redeeming figure that seems neither exactly paternal nor maternal but a fusion of both or beyond both.

15. And much as in *Hamlet* a dramatic teatro mundi, a world of struggles, masks, and paranoia opens around the ghost's appearance.

16. Even though the expression of his departure is a problematic one to the extent that it is not clear that what returns is the same as the one who has left, for it is the ghost of what has left, as if what has left contained an unplaceable excess beyond itself that appears in, or as, the return. The excess that returns seems to belong and not to belong to that which has left. In a way, we might describe Leonardo's procedure as wanting to turn this excess that returns, which we have called the Image, into a Christ, that is, into a figure of a new kind of redemption (and we will discuss later what this might mean), in distinction from Hamlet's father, for example, where it is unclear whether that which returns is a diabolical agent, or not, and in any case is definitely not a redeeming figure but one who at most calls for a vengeful restoration of the world rather than for its transformative redemption. Christ, in Leonardo's interpretation, then, we might say, involves transforming the dimension of the Image from being associated potentially with the negative affects

of the destruction of the world to positive ones, as the redemption of the world. It is only through the ghostly Image qua return from loss of an excess over the paternally centralized world that the world can be transformed and redeemed.

17. Though the landscape is admittedly hard to see due to the damage the painting has suffered through the centuries.

18. I am obviously trying to position the Image as Leonardo conceives it as standing at the threshold between the two sides of what later came to be called nihilism. On the one hand, nihilism as announcing the death of God understood as the annihilation of the metaphysically grounding paternal/theological principle that governed humanity, and on the other hand, a new, positive nihilism, one that announces the nihil, the voiding nothing, as the possibility of a new medium of a humanity no longer grounded in any given center.

19. "God is an infinite sphere, the center of which is everywhere, the circumference nowhere," as the famous saying goes. In the context at hand, we can understand the center that is everywhere as being nothing other than the medium as such, or communication as such, that passes in between everything in its relation to everything else.

20. Emphasis added.

21. All of Leonardo's celebrated figures are holders of secrets, thus essentially related to the question of speech or meaning, but as withheld, as not being yet any specific meaning or utterance. In this sense, his major works are all conceived in relation to the origin of speech or language, the Word (groundless, infinite communication) at the beginning, before any actual words. We can now say that each of Leonardo's major figures serves as a muting encounter through which we are to open up to a new communication. With the exception of the final painting, the enigmatic *St John*, all these muting encounters open us to the landscape.

Chapter Three

1. The "threshold figures" discussed in the Introduction.

2. Much like the interlacing figures, to which we will get, of St Anne and Mary, or the possibly even stranger ones of Leda and the Swan—the swan standing for the intruding stranger.

3. Maurice Merleau-Ponty employs the term "interlace" alongside "intertwining" and "chiasm," especially in the late work *The Visible and the Invisible*. Derrida, for his part, employs it in a brilliant manner in the chapter "Restitutions" in his *The Truth in Painting*.

4. Of course, Christ himself belongs both to the created dimension and the creating one, outside the frame, hence his different position vis-à-vis the two maternal figures. It is as if he allowed for the pictorial system to operate in the first place, connecting the power outside the frame to what is inside, and as such is the inscription within the painting of its very system of operation.

5. We can think of the trinitarian vertical constructions of Rothko in the same pictorial lineage.

6. Those familiar with Lacan cannot help but think of his famous logic of the master signifier (S1), which both belongs and does not belong to the chain of signifiers. It stands for signification itself—the infinite openness of the chain of signification—and is therefore exterior to any particular signifier (S2). In the terminology proposed above, the S1 could be described as a messenger of infinity, in that its task is to keep the chain of signification open. That said, it seems to me that the logic of exceptionality at work in art does not behave in the manner of the S1, which, according to Lacan, follows the law of castration. The S1 prevents any single part of the infinite realm from being associated with a fullness, or potency, of signification. All components of the finite realm are equal to each other in that none of them is complete or autonomous (i.e., they are castrated—like the brothers in Freud's "primal horde"). But the exceptionality of the work of art *is* a matter of potency, gaining and exercising power, even if conceived in terms of creative force (the power received by becoming appropriated to virtual infinity, the non-givenness of worldly order). From the exceptional figure, which we have associated with the term Image, we receive the infinity of the world qua creative force, or a power of originating the world, the power of the Imagination. Through exposure to the exceptional figure, the Image, we gain the power not just to belong, qua equal finite members subjected to the law, to the infinite world, but to participate, qua exceptional members (each one differently, singularly, and unpredictably so), in the creative work of infinity—"worlding," in Heidegger's phrase. In brief, we are dealing here with two kinds of emptiness, or perhaps two sides of emptiness. The negative side (the Law) has to do with limitation, preventing any member of the infinite realm from standing in for an impossible fullness. The other, positive side (Creation) allows for emptiness to be understood, and received, as the creative power of the world to be a groundless and open realm, ceaselessly starting anew. The Image (or perhaps even more the modern image, as Leonardo attempts to develop it qua the liberation of emptiness from any pre-given directionality and formation) is the messenger of infinity (thus a finite-infinite) on which our exceptional participation in the creative opening, origination, and birth of the world depends.

7. *In lieblicher Bläue blühet*
   mit dem metallenen Dache der Kirchthurm. Den umschwebet
   Geschrei der Schwalben, den umgiebt die rührendste Bläue.

In the poem, the replacement of heaven by the landscape is already made at the beginning, through the metaphor of blooming, but only with the opening to the surroundings is the transformation fully effected; on its own, it might seem that the metaphor of blooming suggests a subjection of nature to divine hierarchy.

8. Distinctions and differentiations (e.g., between gestures, facial expressions, types of plants or rocks) are, of course, crucial for Leonardo's sense of realism; that said, they matter to the extent that they give access to the infinite resource of

the world as groundlessly open landscape, out of which an infinity of differences can emerge, singularly and unpredictably. Encountering true, alienating difference means encountering singularity first and foremost: intuition in excess of concept or preconception emerging out of the blue.

9. We are dealing with the breaking of Christian verticality in this context rather than verticality tout court. Leonardo in fact continues to emphasize the significance of verticality, which in many ways constitutes the core enigma in his paintings (as the figure of St Anne attests here, or that of Christ's verticality attested to in *The Last Supper*—or, perhaps most importantly, the figure of St John in Leonardo's last painting, with its celebrated gesture above and beyond the painting). However, such verticality is an enigma emerging in relation to the horizontal context of a landscape, such that the pointing up means not the call to ascend toward the substantial beyond/above as in the medieval St Anne we have examined, but rather is the pointing to the fact that this beyond/above has been evacuated.

10. Not unlike the strange hybrids of figure/images populating the symbolist paintings of Gustave Moreau, such as the famous Oedipus (figure) and the Imaginary Sphinx (image), which is itself a hybrid (which is perhaps more directly reminiscent of Leonardo's Leda and the Swan). As in Leonardo's works, the attached/detached Image is associated with the figure of a riddle, or secret, an enigma of meaning.

11. The interlace is also evident in Mary's clothes. The infinite blue is infused to her through Anne, and through this wrapping she becomes a figure of desire and passion, expressed in the red covering her body and touching her skin. The infinitely blue outside becomes that which possesses the bodily inside. Of course, red passion points to bodily wounding and exposure. This scheme of coloration and the underlying logic goes back to Leonardo's first painting, discussed earlier, *The Annunciation*, where the angel, coming from the blue sky, yet carrying a menacing red of desire and passion, is echoed in the virgin's blue wrapping the still not fully passionate pink, yet which is, so to speak, in its way to full passion.

12. In fact, sacrifice and symbolization belong together. Symbolization is the sacrificial operation through which a real inhabitant of the landscape is made to serve as a relay, or connector, to infinity that is hierarchical and vertical, as it were (hence the centralized location of Van Eyck's lamb, which stands in a vertical line with the celestial dove above it); hereby, true infinity (the unpredictable opening of the world as landscape) is canceled out and transformed into a division between this world and the world above. The symbol marks the transition wherein an occupant of the world is made to serve as representative for a metaphysical order.

Chapter Four

1. Alexander Nagel has pointed to this quality of the close-up in the *Mona Lisa*.

2. Obviously, this decontextualized aspect characterizes almost all portraits. Yet it is clear that Leonardo, in contrast to others who isolate their subject (put-

ting them against a dark background, or a generic open window, for example), is playing with the idea of context here in order to raise questions. He wants us to ask questions about where Mone Lisa is, what exactly her relation to the landscape behind her is, and so on, and as such, by making us question, yet preventing our ability to answer, confronts us more powerfully with her out of place, and out of context nature.

3. A power, and we will also get to this below, which is also always erotic. Eroticism and blankness come together.

4. And one of the speculations regarding the *Mona Lisa* is that she is a woman in mourning, a fact derived, we can see, from her decontextualized position that implies an unnameable loss.

5. As if pregnant with the medium (and we referred above to the speculations regarding Mona Lisa's pregnancy), in the manner of Mary's miraculous pregnancy, where Christ, as we saw in our discussion of both *The Annunciation* and *The Last Supper*, can be understood as the arrival of the medium.

6. In this context, recall the famous close-up in Hitchcock's *Vertigo* (possibly the closest cinematic equivalent we have to the *Mona Lisa* in the complexity of its investigation of the different aspects implicated in the enigmatic portrait of a woman—and the question of the feminine pictorial portrait is of course central to the film) where Scotty (James Stewart) first sees Madeleine (Kim Novak) in the restaurant and is captivated by the glow she radiates, which seems to come from nowhere (relating, incidentally, both the enigmatic artistic shine, and the fetishistic one, having to do with the famous Hitchcockian blonde).

7. Or become visionary, as I called it in a previous book. Becoming visionary is the moment of the reception of, and the appearance of, the power of seeing itself, before and beyond any particular content.

8. One can think of other gestures of the mouth—for instance, the wild laughter that seizes Greta Garbo in *Ninotchka*—which also express satisfaction beyond mirroring, precisely because they are as if caught by an excess beyond any determination which they nevertheless welcome and embrace, subjecting themselves happily to its power.

9. Even if secret content often seems to accrue around the places where the enigma is most active.

10. An exteriority I have called "the off" in my previous book on the cinematic off-screen.

11. Damien Hirst's diamond-covered skull, for example, seems to reflect on this ambiguity.

12. This destabilizing tension between the various elements of the *Mona Lisa's* pose should be distinguished from contrapposto, which Leonardo employs, for example, in *Leda and the Swan*: shifting the center of balance to one side of the body, say a right leg, as in Michelangelo's *David*, and moving other elements so as to complement that center, thus putting the whole formation in a dynamic balance. In the *Mona Lisa*, though it might be said that her left hand is a center

of balance in relation to which the shoulders are positioned in complementary fashion, the whole gestalt is stranger, especially due to the off-center relation of the eyeballs, eyes, face, and shoulder, causing the whole figure to uncannily waver between balance and imbalance, harmony and disharmony. An undercurrent of anxiety and surface resolution results.

13. This is not entirely accurate, for it might be that at first we understand the question regarding our "who" as demanding a contextual response, yet a transformation of this question, as well as of the response to it, comes about when we realize we are those addressed by an enigma. The "who?" question is no longer to be understood as that which requires a response through which we come to occupy a context, but is rather a matter of receiving, or coming to participate in, a power, the power of opening the world within which things have contextual place, the power of the medium.

14. For an analysis of this opening moment of *Hamlet*, see my book *The Off Screen:An Investigation of the Cinematic Frame*, 17–18.

15. There is no more beautiful cinematic moment activating this ambiguity of the maternal call as simultaneously home and exile than the astonishing ending (again, by the sea) of Kenji Mizoguchi's *Sansho the Bailiff,* perhaps the greatest film about the maternal call.

16. To say nothing of a recent auction for "time alone" with her.

17. See Maurice Blanchot's great text, *Le Chant des sirènes.*

18. Chinese paintings, though from the point of view of a different logic, discovered the atmospheric landscape much earlier.

19. And we will get later to the significance of her vampirism, having to do with her being beyond any mirrored reflection.

20. The enigmatic mirror does not reflect, namely, does not present one with oneself as an actuality, but rather effaces one's relation to oneself as an actuality in order to open up "whoness," the exposure to a dimension beyond any actuality. This is why, as Pater observes, the *Mona Lisa* can be thought of as a vampire, that is, as one who is in excess of any reflective mirroring.

Works Cited

Agamben, Giorgio. *Profanations*. New York: Zone Books, 2015.

Arasse, Daniel. *L'Annonciation Italienne*. Paris: Éditions Hazan, 2020.

Barber, Charles. *Contesting the Logic of Painting: Art and Understanding in Eleventh-Century Byzantium*. Boston: Brill, 2007.

Belting, Hans. *Likeness and Presence: A History of the Image before the Era of Art*. Chicago: University of Chicago Press, 1997.

Blanchot, Maurice. *The Siren's Song*. Bloomington: Indiana University Press, 1982.

Clark, Kenneth. *Leonardo da Vinci*. New York: Penguin, 1989.

Cook, Eleanor. "The Figure of Enigma: Rhetoric, History, Poetry." *Rhetorica: A Journal of the History of Rhetoric* 10, no. 4 (2001).

Derrida, Jacques. *The Truth in Painting*. Chicago: University of Chicago Press, 1987.

Fried, Michael. *Absorption and Theatricality*. Chicago: University of Chicago Press, 1988.

Freud, Sigmund. *Leonardo da Vinci and a Memory of His Childhood*. New York: Norton, 1990.

Heidegger, Martin. *Four Seminars*. Bloomington: Indiana University Press, 2003.

Koerner, Joseph Leo. *Bosch and Bruegel: From Enemy Painting to Everyday Life*. The A. W. Mellon Lectures in the Fine Arts, 57.

Koerner, Joseph Leo. "Unmasking the World: Bruegel's Ethnography," *Common Knowledge* 10, no. 2 (2004): 245.

Merleau-Ponty, Maurice. *The Visible and the Invisible*. Evanston, IL: Northwestern University Press, 1968.

Nagel, Alexander. "Leonardo and Sfumato." *RES: Anthropology and Aesthetics* 24: 144

Nancy, Jean-Luc. *Dis-Enclosure: The Deconstruction of Christianity*. New York: Fordham University Press, 2008.

Panofsky, Erwin. *Perspective as Symbolic Form*. New York: Zone Books, 1997.

Pascal, Blaise. *Pensées*. New York: Penguin Classics, 1995.

Pater, Walter. *The Renaissance*. Berkeley: University of California Press, 2020.

Peretz, Eyal. *The Off-Screen: An Investigation of the Cinematic Frame*. Stanford, CA: Stanford University Press, 2017.

Sedgwick, Eve. *Touching Feeling: Affect, Pedagogy, Performativity.* Durham, NC: Duke
    University Press, 2003.
Steinberg, Leo. *Leonardo's Incessant Last Supper.* New York: Zone Books, 2001.
Vasari, Giorgio. *The Lives of the Artists.* Oxford: Oxford University Press, 2008.
Wood, Christopher S. *Albrecht Altdorfer and the Origins of Landscape.* Chicago:
    University of Chicago Press, 1993.

Index